Evaluation
of Peripheral Blood
Lymphocytosis

Evaluation of Peripheral Blood Lymphocytosis

Charles W. Caldwell, M.D., Ph.D.
Professor of Pathology and Anatomical Sciences
University of Missouri School of Medicine
Columbia, Missouri, USA

Francis Lacombe, M.D., Ph.D.
Director of Analytical Cytometry
Hematology Laboratory, Hospital Haut-Lévêque
Pessac, CHU Bordeaux, France

Library of Congress Card Number: 00-109115

ISBN 0-9663422-7-5

Printed in the United States of America

Design and Composition by Hafiz Huda [www.lostpear.com]

Table of Contents

chapter 1

Introduction

Peripheral blood is a commonly analyzed specimen in evaluation of lymphocytosis during presumed infectious or malignant disorders. Therefore, it is important to understand some of the anatomical and physiological features that contribute to alterations in circulating lymphocyte subsets, as well as their distribution in peripheral lymphoid tissues. During lymphocytosis in response to an infectious agent, lymphocytes are continuously being produced in various anatomical sites and are exchanged between sites via the blood and lymphatic systems.

The emergence and disappearance of lymphocyte subsets is thus a dynamic process, and the profile obtained from analysis of blood is a snapshot in time. In many reactive situations, the alterations in peripheral blood reflect mainly changes in lymphocyte trafficking among lymphoid tissues. The immune system of humans is quite interesting and unique in that the components of this system ($\sim 5 \times 10^{11}$ lymphocytes) continuously circulate in blood and lymphatics. Human blood contains only 2% of these cells ($\sim 10^{10}$), while the remaining 98% reside in lymphoid tissues. Thus, any small change in the entry, transit, and exit of lymphocytes from lymphoid tissues will have a significant effect on blood lymphocyte levels. Obviously, this level of sensitivity may not accurately reflect the underlying reactive disorder in tissues. Alterations in lymphocyte numbers may also occur through a number of commonly encountered physiological situations such as stress, circadian rhythm, sleep behavior, and pharmaceutical use.

Decreases of CD4+ T-cells of >30% may occur after just 1 hour of sleep.

In the case of lymphoid malignancies, even a snapshot will usually suffice to characterize the disease, since the lymphocytosis in this case will be chronic and increasing over time.

Peripheral blood lymphocytosis, defined as an absolute increase in circulating lymphoid cells, is a relatively common incidental finding, especially in older age groups. However, since there is an age-related change in the absolute lymphocyte count and in lymphocyte subsets in the blood, it is important to consider age-adjusted normal values when investigating presumed lymphocytosis in children.

Multiple pieces of information are useful in the discrimination of benign versus malignant lymphocytosis, particularly when the absolute lymphocyte count is not dramatically increased. First, data from an automated hematology profile may provide additional clues beyond the observation of lymphocytosis; in the presence of anemia and/or thrombocytopenia, attention should be focused on potential bone marrow disease. The issue of relative versus absolute lymphocytosis is also important. By current definition, neoplastic lymphoproliferative disorders such as B-cell chronic lymphocytic leukemia/small lymphocytic lymphoma (B-cell CLL/SLL) must have an absolute and sustained lymphocytosis. Benign lymphocytoses, however, are most frequently observed as a relative lymphocytosis, or a mild absolute lymphocytosis, and resolve over time.

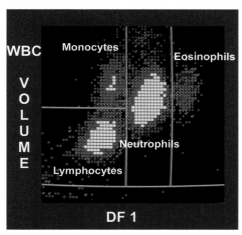

This book is intended to address the common evaluation of peripheral blood lymphocytosis, which can be either a benign, reactive process or indicative of an underlying lymphoid malignancy. The general approach is one of utilizing automated hematology profiling, morphology, and flow cytometry.

Figure 1.1 Screen shot of an automated WBC differential from Coulter® MAXM™.

Approach to Evaluation

At a clinical level, symptoms and physical examination are important for the determination of lymphnode enlargement (lymphadenopathy) and enlargement of the spleen (splenomegaly), (as well as potentially an enlarged thymus in children) as initial steps in evaluation, followed by laboratory examination of the hematology profile and morphology of the peripheral smear.

Figure 1.2 Microscopic morphology remains the cornerstone of diagnosis.

A finding of peripheral lymphocytosis (an absolute lymphocytosis >4000 µL in adults), raises the possibility of a malignant disorder, and becomes a major concern requiring further evaluation. While this also holds true for children (but at a different level of lymphocytes), they do not usually have mature, small lymphoid malignancies. The caveat here is that what may initially appear as small lymphoid cells can sometimes actually be very small, compact blasts in acute myeloid or lymphoid leukemias.

Automated hematology morphologic patterns give strong clues to the appropriate diagnosis.

Indeed, historically, morphology was the only means available for evaluating lymphoproliferative disorders. Although still the cornerstone or all diagnosis, morphology today is usually

Figure 1.3 Screen shot of flow cytometric histograms using Expo32™ software from Beckman Coulter®.

augmented with phenotypic and molecular genetic studies that allow greater consistency and precision in diagnosis.

After an absolute lymphocytosis is established, potential infectious causes should be considered. Is infectious mononucleosis a possibility? If a lymphoproliferative disorder remains a significant possibility after clinical evaluation, cell surface phenotyping of the lymphocytes should be performed.

The value of flow cytometry and immunophenotyping is indisputable in examination of lymphocytosis in order to determine if the expansion is monoclonal or polyclonal, and in the case of neoplastic proliferations, to help characterize and classify the disease. Information on both the percentage of lymphocytes positive for a particular antigen and density of these antigens is obtained. Normal peripheral blood lymphocytes should yield a laboratory-established range of values for normalcy.

Benign Lymphocytosis

Lymphocytosis, particularly in the pediatric population, is most commonly benign and reactive. Benign in this context means that the reaction is polyclonal rather than monoclonal. In reactive lymphocytoses, the morphology is usually different than normal or "resting" lymphocytes.

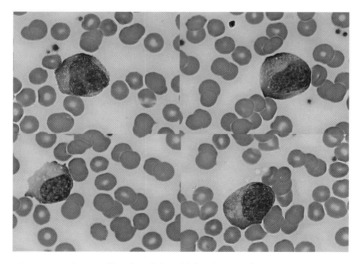

Figure 1.4 Composite of peripheral blood smear from patient with Epstein-Barr virus-related infectious mononucleosis. Wright-Giemsa stain.

Reactive lymphocytes tend to be a more heterogeneous population in terms of both the cytoplasmic and nuclear features. Usually, the cytoplasm will take on a stronger basophilic (blue) staining due mainly to increased mRNA. The nuclei commonly have a finer pattern of chromatin condensation and nuclear outline and nucleoli are sometimes observable. Perhaps the best prototype of reactive lymphocytosis is that of infectious mononucleosis involving Epstein-Barr virus. In this case, most of the reactive cells are actually T-cells that are stimulated by infected B-cells. Viral infections are probably the most common cause of benign reactive lymphocytosis. One non-viral cause, pertussis, produces an interesting pattern that resembles normal lymphocytes more than the "reactive" cells described above. Interestingly, children with pertussis mount a very prominent lymphocytosis, while adults mostly do not. The reasons for this are not clear.

One of the most profound reactive lymphocytoses is observed in CD8+ cells during acute viral infections. These markedly increased cells expressing CD57 and CD8 are commonly observed in infection with HIV, CMV, and EBV, and also occur during the recovery of bone marrow following chemotherapy.

The lymphatic/immune system filters bacteria, viruses, and other foreign substances. When many bacteria or viruses accumulate in one or more lymph nodes, the nodes swell and become quite tender. In general, the nodes affected are those in a particular drainage region of the body. For instance, a sore throat will frequently be accompanied by swollen nodes in the neck (cervical lymph nodes). This swelling is generally the result of producing more lymph node cells, and the cells producing substances that are involved in an immune response to fight off the offending bacteria or virus. This process in termed a reactive hyperplasia, and is not a tumor, but a normal host-defense response of the immune system.

Malignant Lymphocytosis

Lymphoma is a type of cancer that usually develops in the lymph nodes or spleen, which is somewhat paradoxical in that the lymphatic system is mainly responsible for protecting us from infections and tumors. The lymphatic system is comprised of regional collections of small kidney-bean shaped lymph nodes that are connected by a very fine network of lymphatic channels. These collections of nodes are found mainly in the neck (cervical nodes), under the arms (axillary nodes), in the chest (thoracic

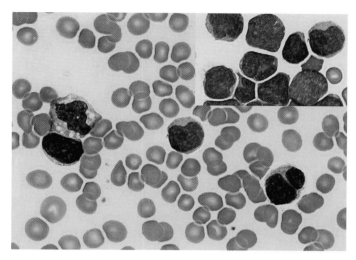

Figure 1.5 Peripheral blood smear from patient with mantle cell lymphoma. The inset is a field from a bone marrow smear. Wright-Giemsa stain.

nodes), in the abdomen (para-aortic nodes) and in the groin. Lymphatic fluid is carried throughout the lymphatic system, including other parts of the immune system such as the spleen, thymus, tonsils, and bone marrow.

Occasionally, something goes awry in the lymphatic system and these normal lymphoid cells become abnormal and start to divide and increase in number uncontrolled. When this happens, a lymphoma develops, and the tumor may then also spread to other lymph nodes and other parts of the body. There are many types of lymphoma that differ in how fast they grow, how they respond to treatment, and in their effects on the body. Two main categories of lymphoma are known, Hodgkin's disease (lymphoma) and non-Hodgkin's lymphomas. Non-Hodgkin's lymphomas (NHL) are further sub-classified based on the type of cell(s) from which they arise in the lymphoid tissues.

Literally any lymphocyte, B or T cell, at any stage of differentiation or activation, is associated with some form of NHL. The classification system(s) that are used to describe NHL will be discussed futher.

Lymphocytosis is associated with only certain types of NHL, and some acute leukemias. Certainly, in the pediatric age group one of the first thoughts is that of Acute Lymphoblastic Leukemia/Lymphoblastic Lymphoma (ALL/LL). While it is true that some cases of ALL present with a lymphocytosis, it is also true that many cases present with cytopenias and low numbers of malignant lymphoblasts in the blood. Cases of ALL/LL of T-cell type are more likely to present with high peripheral blood blast counts.

In adults, ALL/LL can also present with an absolute lymphocytosis, but more commonly cells of more mature differentiation stages produce the lymphocytosis in adults, those related to a "chronic" lymphocytic malignancy, or low-grade lymphoma. Malignant lymphocytoses most commonly show more uniformity in size and nuclear chromatin pattern and frequently show nuclear clefting. (Figure 1.5)

Summary

In this book we will explore some of these issues from a clinical and diagnostic perspective and formulate information for evaluation of reactive versus malignant lymphocytosis and also the discrimination of different malignancies.

Although the illustrations and examples used in this book derive from the use of one hematology analyzer (MAXM) clinical flow cytometer (XL-MCL™) and monoclonal antibodies from Beckman Coulter (Miami, FL), similar patterns may be obtained from other instruments and reagent systems.

chapter **2**

Automated Hematology Instrumentation and Flow Cytometry

The use of automated hematology analyzers has revolutionized the way we practice laboratory medicine. Newer instruments are capable of rapidly examining very large numbers of cells to provide comprehensive hematology profiles. The usual parameters include: WBC, RBC, hemoglobin, hematocrit, RBC indices and measures of cellular variability such as the RDW (red cell distribution width) and MPV (mean platelet volume). In addition, we have become much more aware of the value of automated WBC differential counts.

Most medical technologists perform 100 or 200 cell differential counts, but automated instruments count many more cells in much less time. For instance, the technology developed by Wallace Coulter and subsequently refined over the years, can provide high-quality differential counts of leukocyte subsets and initiate flagging of samples that may be abnormal. Using the COULTER® VCS technology (Volume, Conductivity and Scatter) as one example, in each blood sample > 8,000 leukocytes or 32,000 erythrocytes (RBCs) are directly counted, analyzed and classified. This technology uses direct current (DC) impedance for measuring cell volume, radio frequency (RF) opacity for characterizing the internal composition of each cell, and measurements of light scatter from a coherent helium-neon laser to examine cytoplasmic granularity and nuclear structure.

A brief description of the workings of this analysis system will help in understanding how this technology benefits the laboratorian in initial recognition and analysis of lymphocytosis, or other abnormalities. Hematology analyzers of other manufacturers are also useful in this endeavor, and they utilize some of the same types of measurements, but there are also differences that are beyond the scope and focus of this book for description. Therefore, the example illustrated is that of the Coulter® VCS-based instruments available in our laboratories.

Once the sample is introduced into the instrument, a combination of proprietary reagents and physical agitation in an orbital mixing chamber gently lyses the RBCs, but the WBCs are maintained in what is referred to as a "near native state". The analytical module in the COULTER® VCS-based hematology instruments is a laser-based flow cytometer modified to provide more information on unstained cells than is possible using light scatter alone. A brief description of each parameter may be useful to understand how deviations from normal may be produced by abnormal cells which frequently differ in size, nuclear:cytoplasmic ratio, and other biophysical characteristics.

Volume

Figure 2.1 These VCS-based instruments utilize the Coulter principle of DC impedance to physically measure the volume that each cell displaces in an isotonic diluent. This technique accurately sizes all cell types regardless of their orientation in the light path.

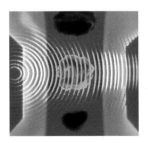

Conductivity

Figure 2.2 Alternating current (AC) in the radio-frequency (RF) range perturbs the bipolar lipid layer of the cell membrane, which then allows the electrical energy to penetrate the cell. This powerful probe provides information about the size of each cell and information on the internal structure and nuclear volume.

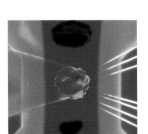

Scatter

Figure 2.3 When a cell enters the beam of a coherent light laser, the scattered light spreads out in all directions. Using a proprietary detector, median angle light scatter (MALS) signals are collected to obtain information about cellular cytoplasmic granularity, nuclear morphometry and cell surface structure.

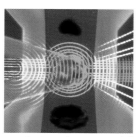

Simultaneous Measurements

Figure 2.4 The VCS-based technology provides a combinatorial single channel analysis utilizing 3 independent energy sources to probe approximately 8,192 cells in their near-native state. In aggregate, these three measurements taken simultaneously provides a high degree of resolution that is used for electronic separation of cells based on multiple characteristics.

Volumetric Compensation

In many optical and electronic measurements, the volume of a cell influences the signal that is generated. For example, a small cell that is a poor conductor can give a signal that is similar to that from a large cell that is a good conductor due to the fact that the energy has to travel farther in the large cell. Similarly, light scatter from 0°-90° is influenced by cellular size; the low angles are the most affected, and indeed are often used as an indirect estimation of cellular size. Since this technology includes an accurate measure of cell volume, this information is used to correct the conductivity and light scatter signals, which results in volumetric compensation that is a very powerful tool for cellular separations. The effect can be seen in Figures 2.5 and 2.6.

Opacity

By correcting the conductivity signal in such a way that it is no longer influenced by cell size, measurements related only to the internal structure of the cell may be made. This method then allows separation of cells of similar size based on differences in internal composition. It also facilitates calculation of the nuclear:cytoplasmic ratio, a feature very useful in distinguishing variant lymphocytes from normal lymphocytes.

Rotated Light Scatter (RLS)

A similar method eliminates the size component of the light scatter signals, and in so doing, enables utilization of light scatter detectors optimized for each cell type covered in the range 10°- 70°. This method facilitates separation of cells such as neutrophils and eosinophils into distinct clusters without mathematical manipulation. It also enhances the separation between the non-granular cell types, such as lymphoid subsets.

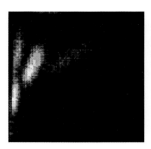

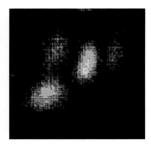

Figure 2.5 Without Volume Compensation.

Figure 2.6 With Volume Compensation.

Three Dimensional Analysis

As each of the > 8,000 WBCs or 32,000 RBCs are analyzed, Volume, Conductivity, Scatter, Opacity and RLS measurements are taken. Each cell is then assigned X, Y and Z coordinates in a 3-dimensional array based respectively on its RLS, Volume and Opacity (Figure 2.7). With the aid of volume compensation, cellular subsets are clearly separated from each other in samples of normal peripheral blood.

Cells with similar VCS characteristics form distinct clusters in this array of over 16 million data points (Figure 2.7). Sophisticated computer software analyzes this clustered data for the number of each member of each cluster and reports a percentage of the total for each cell type. The position in the scattergram is an indicator of morphology.

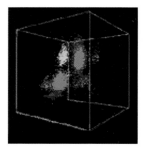

Figure 2.7

Flagging

Spatial deviation of clusters from their normal quantity, shape, position or density are an indication of a distributional or morphological abnormality. A comprehensive set of flags is used to point the medical technologist toward the most likely cause of these abnormalities. Additional sets of user definable flags allow each laboratory to customize their system to achieve optimal efficiency. As shown in Figure 2.8 and 2.9, an apparently deviant lymphocyte population exists, which is 3-dimensionally separated in DF1 and DF2 scattergrams.

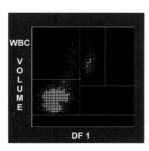

Figure 2.8

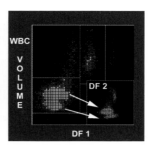

Figure 2.9

The scattergram in Figure 2.10 is from a normal blood sample and illustrates the characteristic position of each cluster in DF1. Note the lymphoid region in the lower-left bounded box and its relatively uniform shape and density. Alterations in the size, the amount of cytoplasm associated with a cell, the complexity of the nucleus in terms of clefting, cleaving, or convolution, and the granularity of the cytoplasm are only some of the cellular characteristics that may produce altered scattergram patterns in the presence of lymphocytoses.

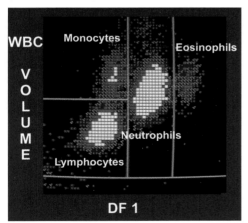

Figure 2.10 Normal scattergram.

A comparison of the normal scattergram with that of samples from reactive and neoplastic lymphocytoses illustrates only a few of the possible alterations that may be produced by abnormal lymphoid cells (Figure 2.11 through 2.16). In some cases, the lymphocytosis causes changes that are mainly numeric, and the scattergram pattern shows only an increase in cells within the lymphoid region with relative decreases in other leukocyte regions. In other cases, the abnormal lymphocytes may coexist with normal lymphocytes and differ enough in VCS characteristics to produce 2 discrete clusters of cells in the lymphoid region. Some cases of lymphocytosis are associated with such cellular heterogeneity within the abnormal population that the lymphoid region becomes less distinct and the scattergram then shows a "blurring" of clusters that cannot be accurately classified on the basis of VCS measurements alone. In certain cases, such as hairy cell leukemia, the abnormal lymphoid cells actually differ from normal enough that they fall into discrete clusters in non- lymphoid regions of the scattergram. All these scattergrams illustrate abnormalities that should be flagged by the instrument as being abnormal in some way; usually as variant lymphocytes or blasts. In all cases, it is necessary to utilize the automated differential and visual inspection of the abnormal scattergram as an initial step in evaluation of lymphocytosis. This should always be followed by morphologic examination of the blood smear to determine if, in fact, these are lymphoid cells, or may be other neoplastic cells such as myeloblasts or lymphoblasts of acute leukemia or high-grade lymphomas.

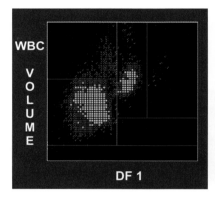

Figure 2.11

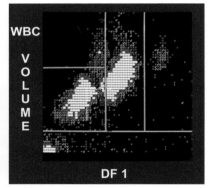

Figure 2.12

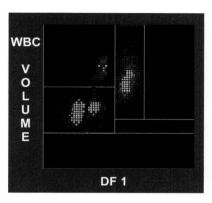

Figure 2.13

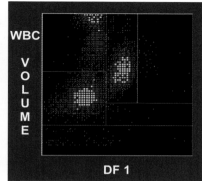

Figure 2.14

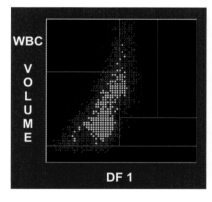

Figure 2.15

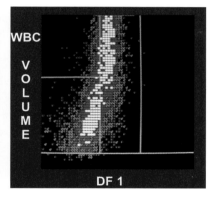

Figure 2.16

Flow Cytometric Analysis

Flow cytometry is clinically useful in many ways. For more details see the excellent clinical flow cytometry texts cited below. In this book, we will focus on pertinent issues relevant to immunophenotyping reactive lymphocytoses versus mature lymphoid leukemias and lymphomas.

Once a lymphocytosis is determined, or suspected from an automated hematology profile and morphologic review of the blood smear, certain questions should be answered:

Will immunophenotyping be medically useful in this clinical setting?

What MoAb panel should be used to define the problem?

Is the lymphoid proliferation benign or neoplastic?

If neoplastic, what is the type and lineage of leukemia or lymphoma?

The answers to these questions should help guide the process of immunophenotyping the lymphocytosis.

Specimen Handling

Optimal collection and transport of blood is essential for high quality immunophenotyping. Without a standardized procedure for sample handling, there is an increased risk of cellular degradation and increased autofluorescence that may hinder flow cytometric analysis. Blood must be collected in an anticoagulant, typically one of three major types

- Acid Citrate Dextrose (ACD)
- Ethylenediamino-tetraacetic acid (EDTA)
- Sodium Heparin
- Any of these should maintain cell viability and CD expression for at least 24-48 hours when stored at room temperature.

Since the intent is to characterize a lymphocytosis, cellularity should not be a problem. Nevertheless, in such a setting, consider the clinical questions to be answered and choose the MoAbs that attempt to answer the most medically significant questions.

Some laboratories use density gradients such as Ficoll, while others use whole blood lysis (WBL) methods. It should be pointed out that most low grade and intermediate grade lymphomas and reactive lymphocytoses will yield representative cell suspensions, with or without density gradient separation. While WBL is preferred, the ability to maintain a native cellular state is not always possible. The cells being stained with MoAbs to Igs will need to be "washed" prior to antibody addition to eliminate free plasma immunoglobulin.

The technologist may also need to adjust high cell concentrations down with dilution in order to avoid antigen excess. Viability is usually not an issue, but the utilization of a vital dye such as 7 Aminoactinomycin D (7 AAD) may be helpful to identify non viable cells.

Flow Cytometric Identification of Cells of Interest

A central issue in flow cytometry is the characterization of the cell type(s) of interest, based on cellular gating. Such gating strategies are essential for accurate immunophenotyping, particularly when there is a heterogeneous cell suspension and/or the target cell population is present in a low percentage. In the setting of mature lymphoid leukemias and related lymphomas, the cell types that need to be definable are usually:

- Mature lymphocytes
- Large lymphoid cells (or blasts)
- Plasmacytoid cells

Further, the cells are usually not few in number in the case of lymphocytosis. Correlation of light scatter gating and immunophenotypic pattern with the original specimen and/or cell suspension by morphology is critical in identifying the small minority of cases where these standard gating protocols fail to detect the cells of interest.

The flow cytometric identification of lymphoid cells is often accomplished by light scatter gating (Figure 2.17). This is most reliably done when dealing with lymphocytosis, where the benign and/or malignant lymphocytes comprise the majority of all cells. Difficulties with pure light scatter gating occur typically in cases with a low percentage of neoplastic cells. One other specific difficulty in using light scatter gating is with Hairy Cell Leukemia, where the cells are larger, have more forward (and side) scatter, and fall more into the region normally occupied by monocytes or large lymphocytes.

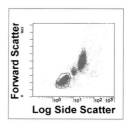

Figure 2.17 Flow cytometric histogram of forward angle (y-axis) versus log side (x-axis) light scatter of a whole blood specimen.

In the case of lymphocytosis, the most useful CDs to direct gating for neoplastic cells are CD45, CD19/20 or CD3. CD45 immunofluorescence is usually bright on benign and malignant mature lymphoid cells. Thus, gating on the brightly CD45 positive / low side light scatter cluster is fairly specific for mature T, B and NK lymphoid cells.

The flow cytometric identification of plasma cells is more difficult than lymphocytes, as the plasma cells lack certain CD antigens such as CD19, 20, 22, 45, and sIg. In the context of lymphocytosis, plasma cell malignancies are very uncommon. However, lymphoplasmacytic lymphomas frequently circulate. These typically express B-cell and plasma cell CDs simultaneously.

The two most common antigens used in plasma cell identification are CD38 and CD138. CD38 is sensitive, but nonspecific. CD138 is not always present on malignant plasma cells or expressed dimly on only a fraction of these cells, thus it is perhaps more specific, but less sensitive.

Immunophenotyping Panels.

The choice of diagnostic antibodies is based upon the clinical question to be answered. The question(s) of differentiation and/or clonality may be answered by the same set of MoAbs.

In reactive lymphocytoses, it may be necessary to utilize both T- and B-cell CDs for characterization. Most mature lymphoid leukemias and lymphomas are of B lineage, in North America and Europe. Thus, in the absence of features of T cell differentiation it is reasonable to focus more on B-cell CDs and clonality. T-cell vs. B-cell lineage can be reliably determined with "pan" T cell antigens CD3 and CD5 along with a reliable B lineage marker such as CD19 or CD20.

Some laboratories prefer CD19 over CD20 as a "pan" B-cell CD used for gating. CD19 antigen is distinctly present on virtually all mature B-cell leukemias and lymphomas and is specific. The CD20 antigen has less sensitivity and specificity. It is dimly expressed on a variable minority of T cells in both blood and marrow, and rarely on T-cell lymphomas. However, many laboratories find little difference between CD19 and CD20 in practice. Some use the discrepancy in %-positive CD19 versus CD20 to help discern B-cell chronic lymphocytic leukemia/small lymphocytic lymphoma (B-CLL/SLL), where CD20 is often dimly expressed whereas CD19 is normally expressed.

The definition of mature T-cells revolves about expression, or lack of expression, of pan-T-cell antigens. The choice of CD5 as a T cell marker is appropriate only when combined with a specific B-cell CD. This is due to the frequent presence of CD5+ B-CLL/SLL and mantle cell lymphoma (MCL). CD19+ / CD5+ cells are of B lineage, while CD19 - / CD5 + cells are presumed to be T-cell lineage. CD3 is a good marker of T-cell lineage. Nevertheless, definition of a neoplastic lymphocytosis generally involves the loss of one or more pan-T-cell CDs. Sometimes, flow cytometry alone is not sufficient to determine T-cell clonality, and molecular methods become necessary.

Immunoglobulin light chain expression (sIg, cIg) is critical in the assessment of B-cell clonality. Reactivity with anti-kappa and -lambda should be assessed by a multicolor method in order to accurately determine that it is only B-cells that are being evaluated since non-specific binding can occur. Flow cytometry laboratories accredited by the College of American Pathologists (CAP) are required to use techniques to differentiate between specific membrane bound sIg from non-specific immunoglobulin binding via Fc receptors.

Sometimes there is no clear separation between the light chain positive and negative B-cells due to very dim expression below the level of sensitivity.

No single approach to light chain analysis is successful in all instances of B-cell leukemia or lymphoma, and a combined approach with multicolor kappa/lambda/pan-B CD, using either light scatter and/or B-cell gating for identification, is probably the most effective method.

Sometimes, additional markers are indicated by the initial clinical and morphologic impressions. Typically, this includes MoAbs to CD5, CD10, CD23, and either CD11c or CD103. One may also include FMC7 and/or CD25 in the primary panels, particularly if using a 3 or 4 color setup. While CD20, CD22 and CD79b are not favored for B-cell identification, their inclusion in panels is deemed appropriate by some laboratories for accurate differentiation of B-CLL/SLL from other mature B-cell lymphoproliferations.

A more extensive T-cell panel is usually not indicated unless a T-cell malignancy is suggested by other data. In such instances, a broadened panel directed at T-cell antigens is appropriate. Usually, these will include all major "pan" T- cell CDs (CD2, 3, 5, 7), CD4 and CD8. Depending upon the degree of prior clinical and morphologic evaluation, NK antigens (CD16, 56, 57) and/or CD25 may be included.

Interpretation

Diagnosis of mature lymphoid neoplasms includes automated hematology panels, morphologic evaluation, and immunophenotypic, and other laboratory data. The person interpreting data should begin with a careful review of the cellular identification gate(s), and the resultant immunofluorescence plots and the cutoffs used to define the percentages of antigen positive and negative cells.

In many laboratories, when malignancy is identified, the CDs are each given a "positive" or "negative" assignment. There is no consensus on the threshold for positivity. Most laboratories use a value of 10-30% of the malignant cells that must express each CD to be considered "positive". The quantitation of the fraction of antigen positive cells becomes more difficult if the fluorescence peaks of the positive and negative populations overlap due to dim staining. Interpretation in these cases is difficult.

Careful consideration of the immunophenotypic profile can aid in the interpretation of dim immunofluorescence staining. One should expect to see a pattern of both positive and pertinent negative CDs that aid in the final interpretation.

Reactive, or polyclonal, lymphocytoses should be reported as such, while in the case of lymphoid malignancy, an immunophenotype should be described, along with an appropriate diagnostic interpretation that takes into account morphology, as well as other laboratory data.

References

Flow Cytometry and Clinical Diagnosis (2nd edition)
David F. Keren, Curtis A. Hanson, Paul E. Hurtubise, Eds.,
American Society of Clinical Pathologists Press, Chicago, 1994,
ISBN 0-89189-346-6.

Flow Cytometry: Clinical Applications
Marion G. Macey, Blackwell Scientific Publications, Oxford, 1994,
ISBN 0-632-03673-7.

Clinical Flow Cytometry: Principles & Application
Kenneth D. Bauer, Ricardo E. Duque, T. Vincent Shankey,
Williams & Wilkins, Baltimore, 1993, ISBN 0-683-00480-8.

Clinical Applications of Flow Cytometry
Roger S. Riley, Edwin J. Mahin, William Ross, Igaku-Shoin Press,
New York, 1993. ISBN 0-89640-200-2.

chapter **3**

Monoclonal Antibodies and Analyte Specific Reagents

O ver the years in research laboratories, huge numbers of different monoclonal antibody (MoAb) clones have been produced, many of which were quite similar in their reactivity/specificity. The First International Workshop on Leukocyte Differentiation Antigens examined various different clones, and MoAb specificities determined to be the same were grouped into what became known as cluster designations (CD). The aim was to standardize nomenclature and establish a form of equivalency. These workshops played an exceedingly important role in characterizing the performance of these biological reagents through detailed chemical and physical studies, and, more importantly, their cellular patterns of reactivity on both normal and malignant cells.

Most clinically useful MoAbs are classified into CDs, with a few exceptions. One of the purposes of the international workshops was to examine many MoAb clones from many laboratories around the world and to determine those that reacted similarly with the same target antigens. In this way, it was hoped that MoAb clones that were the same (or very similar) could be used interchangeably and the terminology could be simplified to CD nomenclature. For the most part, this has been a very successful approach. In the case of clinical diagnosis, it should be noted that not all MoAb clones from the same CD have exactly the same reactivity. However, published data show that these differences should not be clinically important.

Summarized information on clinically useful MoAbs for evaluating lymphocytoses is found in the Appendix to this book. In addition, useful information about surface molecules, MoAbs, and their reactivity can be found via the Internet at PROW, Proteins Reviews on the Web (http://www.ncbi.nlm.nih.gov/prow).

Analyte Specific Reagents

In the United States, but not other parts of the world, one issue now affecting the practice of clinical flow cytometry in classifying neoplastic cells is the need for validation of MoAbs that are classified as analyte specific reagents, or ASRs. Though there is clear guidance regarding the validation of laboratory tests of certain types, a number of questions remain unanswered with respect to validation of MoAbs (ASRs) in diagnosis of leukemia and lymphoma. In part, this is due to the biologically variable nature of the analytes in question: cellular proteins. Laboratories have used MoAbs for this purpose for years, but recent actions by the U.S. Food and Drug Administration (FDA) have led to a requirement for laboratories to address the validation process specifically in this area.

The FDA holds authority over commercialization of diagnostic products as they pertain to health care. Commercial providers of reagents such as MoAbs typically perform clinical trials to provide evidence of equivalence for new versus existing products under the 510(k) premarket notification process. When deemed equivalent and otherwise appropriate, the FDA allows manufacturers to market these reagents for in vitro diagnostic (IVD) use. In some cases, such as leukemia and lymphoma immunophenotyping, no IVD MoAbs were available for the intended use. Laboratories then used "unapproved" MoAbs for medical diagnosis, or used IVD MoAbs in combinations or in methods that rendered them no longer IVD-approved.

The Immunology Devices Panel proposed rules to regulate ASRs, and following a comment period, the FDA published the final rule for ASRs on November 21, 1997, which became effective on November 23, 1998. The FDA regards ASRs as laboratory reagents comprising chemicals or antibodies that are "active ingredients" of tests used to identify one specific disease or condition.

Specific issues need to be addressed when using MoAbs labeled as ASRs by manufacturers.

- Sale of ASRs is now restricted to laboratories designated under the Clinical Laboratory Improvement Amendments (CLIA) of 1988 as qualified to perform high-complexity testing.

- Only physicians and other health care practitioners authorized by applicable state law can order the use of in-house developed tests using ASRs.

The rule also specifically requires laboratories to include a disclaimer with results obtained through the use of tests incorporating ASRs. The disclaimer must read as follows: "This test was developed and its performance characteristics determined by [Laboratory Name]. It has not been cleared or approved by the U.S. Food and Drug Administration."

The FDA allows inclusion of additional clarifying language in the report, as long as the required disclaimer is present. Language suggested by the College of American Pathologists (CAP) might include: "The FDA has determined that such clearance or approval is not necessary. This test is used for clinical purposes. It should not be regarded as investigational or for research."

To be in compliance with the final rule, flow cytometry laboratories should have policies and procedures to document the validation of individual, or combinations (panels) of, ASRs (MoAbs) for use in characterizing leukemias and lymphomas prior to their use in patient testing.

One issue to address in validation is determination of the flow cytometric "test" to be validated. The FDA states that ASRs are "used to identify one specific disease or condition." Since individual MoAbs are of limited use in this regard, and the standard of practice is to use panels of reagents for characterizing leukemias and lymphomas, one approach might be to make the "test" (ASR) the composite panel of reagents and then validate the combinations, or panels, of MoAbs used in the laboratory for their intended purpose.

Potential components of a validation protocol might include:

- Peer-reviewed literature to support use of specific ASRs or combinations of ASRs

- CLIA requirements, as applicable, for test validation

- Results of flow cytometry proficiency surveys

- Correlative morphologic information from cytology/histology
- Ancillary testing results such as cytochemical staining or molecular diagnostics

Pertinent peer-reviewed literature might include journal articles that reference the clones used for clinical testing, potentially with outcomes of their use. Additionally, pertinent clinical reviews might include that of Jennings and Foon on immunophenotypic evaluation of leukemias and lymphomas and papers comprising the US-Canadian Consensus Conference Recommendations, and, for those clones that have been examined through the international workshops, the appropriate volume of the proceedings of the workshops.

The CLIA document addresses validation of test procedures using non-IVD reagents developed after September 1, 1992. There are stated requirements to verify or establish laboratory methods. Similar items are covered in the CAP Laboratory General Inspection Checklist and the Flow Cytometry Inspection Checklist.

Pertinent to the validation process, Sub-Part K, 493.1213 of the Clinical Laboratory Improvement Amendments of 1988 (CLIA) ("Establishment and verification of method performance specifications"), states that "prior to reporting patient test results", the laboratory should "verify or establish for each method the performance specifications for the following performance characteristics, as applicable."

This paragraph specifies the attributes of validation of general laboratory tests, but not all are necessarily applicable to all tests, such as leukemia and lymphoma immunophenotyping. Included in the validation process are:

- Accuracy
- Precision
- Analytical sensitivity
- Analytical specificity (to include interferences)
- Reportable range of results
- Reference range
- Any other performance characteristic required for test performance

The first issue to address in implementing this approach in flow cytometry is determination of what is applicable. As an example, validation of ASRs for immunophenotyping leukemia/lymphoma might be viewed in the following manner:

- Accuracy (applicable, if the test is a panel and the purpose is lineage identification)

- Precision (not applicable)

- Analytical sensitivity (applicable, if sensitivity is defined as detection of dimly expressed antigens necessary for a composite immunophenotypic characterization)

- Analytical specificity (applicable, if specificity is defined as specific lineage identification)

- Reportable range of results (not applicable)

- Reference range (not applicable)

- Any other performance characteristic required for test performance (applicable, discussed below)

Sub-Part H specifies that "All laboratories must enroll in a proficiency testing (PT) program that has been approved by HHS (Health and Human Services). The laboratory must test PT samples just as patient samples." This may be addressed by participation in the CAP Flow Cytometry Survey Sets (FL) and Leukemia/Lymphoma Survey FL3, or equivalent approved programs. Successful participation is another element to document in a prospective fashion the validity of an individual laboratory's ASRs (panels) compared with other laboratories using similar or dissimilar methods.

Correlation of flow cytometric data with cytology/histology is particularly important in the validation of ASRs used in immunophenotyping malignancies such as leukemias and lymphomas. Morphology and histology observations will determine if a malignancy is present (at diagnosis). Morphology of cytocentrifuge-prepared cell samples will also determine if representative malignant cells are present if a density gradient separation method is employed. As a validation tool, the morphology may be used to support the interpretation of the flow cytometric data.

Because the validation process is being initiated after the fact, and these MoAbs have been used clinically for some time, what is the role of retrospective data? Most laboratories now have historical data and comparisons are available for cytology/histology results and lymphoma classifications that can help in validation and even in clinical outcome assessments.

Therefore, building case files, particularly in the area of leukemia and lymphoma, can help validate the methods and reagents retrospectively, provided the panels (ASRs) have not changed.

One example of validation might involve something named "Lymphocytosis Panel."

ASR Name: Lymphocytosis Panel

Intended Use: Identification and assignment of cell lineage in peripheral blood lymphocytosis.

Date of Implementation: November 12, 2000.

Composition of the ASR			
Tube #	FITC	PE	ECD
1	Kappa	Lambda	CD19
2	FMC7	CD23	CD19
3	CD5	CD10	CD19
4	CD20	CD10	CD19
5	CD103	CD11c	CD19
6	CD16	CD56	CD3
7	CD5	CD7	CD3
8	CD8	CD4	CD3
9	Negative	Negative	CD45

Manufacturer of ASRs: IoTest 3, Beckman Coulter, Miami, FL

Accuracy: This panel (ASR) accurately determined the cell lineage in 74/75 cases of mature B-cell and T-cell lymphomas and in 55/55 cases of non-neoplastic, polyclonal lymphocytosis.

Precision: Not applicable.

Analytical Sensitivity: Not applicable. This test is not quantitative, but used only to identify the cell lineage of neoplastic lymphocytes, or to rule out the presence of clonality.

Analytical Specificity:

- B-cell CLL/SLL, as defined by histology and ancillary testing, shows 25/25 cases correct.

- B-cell MCL, as defined by histology and ancillary testing, shows 25/25 cases correct.
- T-cell Sezary Syndrome, as defined by histology of skin biopsies and ancillary testing, shows 24/25 cases positive (see "Corrective Action" for explanation).

Reportable Range: Not applicable.

Reference Range: Not applicable.

Other Performance Characteristics Required for Test Performance:

- Use of 20 microliters of each MoAb reagent with 100 microliters blood.
- Use whole blood lysis procedure with Multi-QPrep™ (Beckman Coulter)
- Correlation with cytology/morphology/histochemistry (74/75 cases agreed).
- Correlation with outside referrals (agreed with 15/15 Cancer and Leukemia, Group B (CALGB) referrals).

Proficiency Surveys (CAP):

This panel correctly assigned the cell lineage to:
B-cell CLL/SLL (FL3-04, 2000)

This panel incorrectly assigned lineage to: None

Corrective Action: This case of Sezary Syndrome had very low numbers of circulating cells, and was of an unusual immunophenotype with CD7+ cells. The laboratory was made aware of the possibility of this immunophenotype and the need for morphology/histology correlations.

Pertinent Literature:

Jennings CD, Foon KA. Recent advances in flow cytometry: application to the diagnosis of hematologic malignancy. Blood. 1997;90:2863-2892. (Discusses immunophenotypes of specific acute leukemias.)

Stewart CC, Behm FG, Carey JL, et al. U.S.-Canadian consensus recommendations on the immunophenotypic analysis of hematologic neoplasia by flow cytometry: selection of antibody combinations. Cytometry (Comm Clin Cytometry). 1997;30:231-235. (Addresses composition of panels for acute leukemias.)

Specific workshop citations regarding MoAb clone reactivity.

Data to support these statements should be stored for retrieval when needed. The validation document(s) will likely be dynamic, and updated periodically to reflect additional cases and supportive data. Validation will also need to be updated as components of the panel (ASR) are changed.

References

Medical Devices; Classification/Reclassification; Restricted Devices; Analyte Specific Reagents. 21 CFR 809. Final rule. Federal Register 62:62243–62260 (1997).

College of American Pathologists, Commission of Laboratory Accreditation. Flow Cytometry Inspection Checklist, 1997.0. Northfield, Ill: College of American Pathologists; 1997.

College of American Pathologists, Commission of Laboratory Accreditation. Laboratory General Inspection Checklist, 1996.2. Northfield, Ill: College of American Pathologists; 1996.

Borowitz MJ, Bray R, Gascoyne R, et al. U.S.-Canadian consensus recommendations on the immunophenotypic analysis of hematologic neoplasia by flow cytometry: data analysis and interpretation. Cytometry (Comm Clin Cytometry). 1997;30:236–244.

Braylan RC, Atwater SK, Diamond L, et al. U.S.-Canadian consensus recommendations on the immunophenotypic analysis of hematologic neoplasia by flow cytometry: data reporting. Cytometry (Comm Clin Cytometry). 1997;30:245–248.

Rothe G, Schmitz G. Consensus protocol for the flow cytometric immunophenotyping of hematopoietic malignancies: working group on flow cytometry and image analysis. Leukemia. 1996;10:877–895.

Stewart CC, Behm FG, Carey JL, et al. U.S.-Canadian consensus recommendations on the immunophenotypic analysis of hematologic neoplasia by flow cytometry: selection of antibody combinations. Cytometry (Comm Clin Cytometry). 1997;30:231–235.

Jennings CD, Foon KA. Recent advances in flow cytometry: application to the diagnosis of hematologic malignancy. Blood. 1997;90:2863–2892.

chapter 4

Lymphocyte Production and Differentiation

To understand how and why a lymphocytosis occurs in benign, reactive circumstances, and these same cell types can also occur in malignancies, it is helpful to understand the origins of these cells, and some of the reasons they proliferate.

Introduction

The usual job of lymphoid cells in the body is host defense; to fight intrusions by microbial organisms and tumors. It is easy to see why such cells might then be increased during times of microbial challenge. That is, when the body detects a need for more immune cells to help fight off a potential infection, the bone marrow is capable of expanding production of early lymphoid precursors, and the peripheral lymphoid organs are capable of undergoing expansion as well. This may involve any/all subsets of lymphocytes. Such processes can be viewed as a lymphoid hyperplasia, an expansion of lymphoid tissues and hence, circulating lymphocytes.

Understanding normal development of B-cells and T-cells will help in understanding issues related to the small B-cell and T-cell lymphomas/leukemias, which are commonly associated with peripheral blood lymphocytosis in adults. Various stages of B-cell and T-cell development present particular morphologic, immunologic, and genotypic patterns that can be exploited in evaluation of benign and malignant lymphocytoses. We will explore some of the reasons why peripheral blood lymphocyte levels are affected by changes within lymphoid tissues.

The Anatomy of the Lymphoid System

The lymphoid system is unique; its component cells are not confined to a single organ, but are in continuous circulation throughout the body. Lymphocytes differ from other leukocytes in that they not only leave the blood and enter tissues, but also recirculate continuously back to the blood via lymphatics, thus ensuring maintenance of consistent immuno-logic surveillance throughout the body. The immune system utilizes both the blood and lymphatic circulations to maintain a continuous system. This relationship is important to the body's host-defense mechanisms, as lymphoid tissue filters out micro-organisms capable of causing disease, produces certain white blood cells, and produces antibodies.

There are also certain anatomic sites where the cells of the lymphoid system are organized into specific structures (Figure 4.1) These are:

- Central lymphoid tissues (bone marrow, thymus)
- Peripheral lymphoid tissues (lymph nodes, spleen, mucosa-associated lymphoid tissue)

The central lymphoid tissues are mainly responsible for producing immature B- and T-cells that have not been exposed to antigens, while the peripheral lymphoid tissues are where antigen encounters occur and secondary changes to lymphocytes ensue.

The lymphatic system is also important for the distribution of fluids and nutrients in the body, because it drains excess fluids and protein so that tissues do not swell up. Lymph is a body fluid which clots like blood and flows unidirectionally toward peripheral lymph nodes because valves prevent back flow under normal physiological conditions. Lymph capillaries merge into larger lymphatics which drain into lymph nodes. The efferent lymph from regional lymph nodes may also drain into one or more additional nodes before flowing into major efferent lymphatics. The lymphatic vessels are present wherever there are blood vessels. Numerous tiny oval lymph nodes are present mainly in the neck, groin and axillae, but also scattered along the lymphatics. They act as barriers to infection by filtering out and destroying toxins and microorganisms. The largest single mass of lymphoid tissue in the human body is the spleen.

Central Lymphoid Tissues

Bone Marrow

All T- and B- cells, mononuclear phagocytes, platelets, erythrocytes, and other leukocytes originate in the bone marrow. The aggregate volume and weight of this tissue is quite large, surpassing that of the liver. There is a normal, progressive hematopoietic cell maturation from immaturity in areas near bone to mature differentiation the interface with vessels. It is mainly the differentiated cells that lie along the dilated vascular channels into which they will pass. The marrow monitors and controls release of hematopoietic cells to the peripheral blood by mechanisms that remain unclear.

Both T- and B-cells are normally present within bone marrow aspirates and biopsies. In adults, the marrow cellularity normally contains <15% lymphocytes, and these are mainly mature T-cells, with only 5-15% B-cells. The ratio of CD4:CD8 is commonly reversed in bone marrow compared to peripheral blood. The situation is different in pediatrics. Children normally have fewer T-cells, but have an increased population of immature B-cells and B-cell precursors in the bone marrow, the proportions of each changing inversely with age. These early precursor B-cells are sometimes referred to as "hematogones" and express "immature" cell-surface antigens such as HLA-Dr, CD19, CD10, and CD20. Morphologically, they appear as small compact lymphocytes (Figures 4.2 and 4.3).

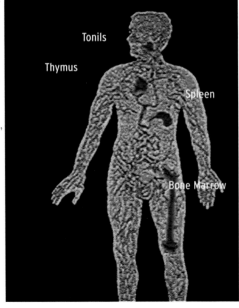

Figure 4.1 Illustration of major lymphoid areas and lymphatics.

The first stage of differentiation of B-cell progenitors in the bone marrow is assembly of genes for the variable (V) regions of the immunoglobulin (Ig) heavy and light chains through a process termed V(D)J recombination. DNA located between the rearranging gene segments is deleted from the chromosome. The V-region genes of the light chains (which can be of κ or λ type) are assembled from V and joining (J) elements. Those of the heavy chains are assembled from V, diversity (D), and J elements. There are many different V, D, and J segments in the human germ line, thus each B-cell generates a specific pair of genes for its heavy-chain V region and another pair for its light-chain V region. These differ from those of all other B-cells and each encodes a distinct antibody. These distinct gene rearrangements also equip each B-cell with individual molecular clonal markers – a feature essential for the analysis of B-cell lymphomas/leukemias based on clonality.

The expression of surface Ig (sIg) as an antigen receptor of B-cells is critically important for the development and survival of B-cells. In development, the cells go through an ordered program of V(D)J rearrangements in which the only surviving cells are those that have acquired heavy- and light-chain V-region genes that can be translated into protein. Cells that cannot, undergo apoptotic cell death, a programmed process. In mature B-cells, the expression of sIg is also essential for survival, because induced deletion of the antigen receptor in vivo leads to rapid cell death.

Receptor specificity is crucial for B-cells throughout their lifespan. In the bone marrow, newly formed B-cells expressing autoreactive sIg either undergo apoptosis or "edit" their receptors by means of secondary V(D)J rearrangements. Once this process of receptor editing (mostly resulting in the replacement of one light chain by another) leads to the expression of an "innocent" B-cell receptor, the B-cell leaves the bone marrow to become a mature, naive (not yet exposed to any antigen) B-cell. Modification in the specificity of the B-cell antigen receptor by genetic means is resumed in a later phase of B-cell differentiation in peripheral lymphoid tissue germinal centers in the course of T-cell-dependent immune responses. These stages are shown in Figure 4.3.

At least 3 stages of B-cell development are immunophenotypically discernable in the bone marrow:

- Pre-pre-B-cells (cIgM-)
- Pre-B-cells (cIgM+)
- Virginal small B-cells (usually sIgM+/IgD+)

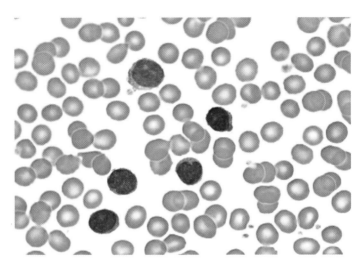

Figure 4.2 Hematogones in Peripheral Blood, Wright-Giemsa stain.

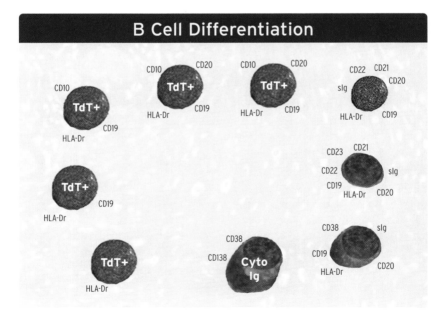

Figure 4.3 Putative stages of B-cell differentiation.

These virginal small B-cells then go on to circulate in the blood until they eventually populate the marginal zones of lymphoid follicles in peripheral lymphoid tissues. One reason to address this group of precursor B-cells in the context of peripheral blood lymphocytosis is that these cells may in fact circulate in blood under certain circumstances of physiological stress and mimic early neoplastic conditions (Figure 4.2). Pre-T-cells are also produced in the bone marrow, and travel to the thymus where they undergo further differentiation.

Thymus

The thymus (Figure 4.4) is present in the anterior part of the chest, or mediastinum, and is an encapsulated, lobulated organ divided into 2 anatomically distinct regions:

- A cortex that is densely populated with lymphocytes and
- The medulla, which appears more epithelial because of a relative paucity of lymphoid cells.

The thymus provides a friendly microenvironment for bone marrow-derived pre-T cells to enter, clonally expand, acqurie antigen and major histocompatibility (MHC) haplotype specificities, differentiate, and exit to the peripheral lymphoid organs. Approximately 90-95% of these cells die in the thymic cortex, while the remaining 5-10% undergo further differentiation. The surviving cells represent T-cells capable of antigen recognition on antigen-presenting cells (APC), but do not recognize "self" components.

The route of traffic of pre-T cells to specific regions of the thymus and out again has long been debated and the controversy remains. The prevailing dogma is that pre-T cells multiply in the cortex, begin to mature and then migrate toward the medulla where recirculating cells exit via postcapillary venules near the corticomedullary junction and non-recirculating cells exit via efferent lymphatics in the capsule and inter-lobular septae.

The thymus in children is much larger than in adults relative to total body size. As an individual matures, the thymus undergoes a process of shrinkage or atrophy referred to as involution. In humans, involution begins around the onset of puberty. Even so, the thymus remains function-al throughout life.

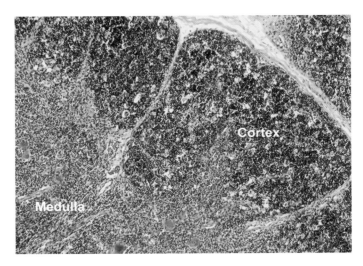

Figure 4.4 Histologic section of thymus, H + E stain.

The function of the T-cell receptor (TCR) for antigen is analogous to that of membrane Ig in B-cells. Immediately after commitment to the T-cell lineage, immature thymocytes undergo rearrangement of TCRγ, TCRδ, and TCRβ genes. Cells that have productively rearranged TCRγ and TCRδ then express the γ/δTCR complex. Rearrangement of TCRβ alone produces a pre-TCR+ thymocyte, and at the CD4+/CD8+ stage, rearrangement of αTCR then results in a mature α/βTCR complex. The TCR is comprised of paired polypeptides (α/β or γ/δ) associated in the membrane with CD3 and certain accessory molecules such as CD4, CD8 and CD2.

The T-cell progenitor termed the prothymocyte has not yet rearranged the TCR genes, but expresses cell-surface CD7, CD2, CD38, and CD71. These surface molecules have certain functions, including transferrin binding (CD71) and intercellular adhesion (CD2). These least mature T-cells reside in the thymic cortex. At the next stage, the thymocyte, cells gain CD1, CD5, and co-express CD4 and CD8. A small proportion of these cells are CD5-, and represent natural killer cells.

Mature T-cells leave the thymus when they lose surface expression of CD38 and commit to single expression of CD4 or CD8 at which time the cells become immunocompetent and populate secondary lymphoid tissues. A separate population of CD3+ T-cells are negative for both CD4 and CD8, and have rearranged γ and δ TCR genes. These cells are found primarily in skin and intestine.

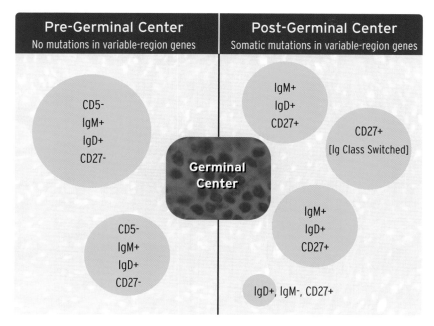

Figure 4.5 Immunophenotypic changes associated with pre- and post-germinal center maturation.

Other than advanced stages of lymphoblastic lymphomas, the vast majority of T-cell malignancies that circulate in blood are of mature phenotypes. These are uncommon diseases with a much higher incidence in adults over children.

Peripheral or Secondary Lymphoid Tissues

Whereas primary lymphoid tissues produce early T- and B-cell precursors, secondary lymphatic tissues control the quality of immune responses. Naïve B-cells (usually sIgM+/sIgD+) comprise about 60% of peripheral blood B-cells, circulate through the blood, and then populate lymphoid tissues for further differentiation. These cells, which in contrast to memory B cells usually carry somatically unmutated genes and do not express the CD27 surface marker (Figure 4.5), can be subdivided into CD5- and CD5+IgM+IgD+ B cells, the former being the presumed precursors of germinal-center B cells. About 15 percent of peripheral-blood B cells are CD5+ B cells. Secondary lymphoid organs contain naive CD5-

IgM+IgD+CD27- cells, along with CD5+ B cells, in primary follicles and in the mantle zone of secondary follicles. Normally, a portion of inner mantle zone B-cells will express CD5. These mantle zone cells are considered "pre-follicular", but once they go on to enter the follicular center, they become transformed follicular center cells losing IgD and either maintain IgM or undergo class switching to another heavy chain. Following the process of antigen engagement and selection, these become cleaved cells or centrocytes, many of which express CD10. Adjacent to the mantle zone is the postfollicular marginal zone which may contain parafollicular or monocytoid B cells. These cells typically have rather abundant pale blue cytoplasm. Marginal zone cells are typically IgM+. Additional postfollicular marginal zone cells might include recirculating memory B cells} and plasma cells.

Genotypically, prefollicular B-cells have rearranged, but non-mutated Ig genes. However, once the cells move into the follicular center, they undergo somatic mutations that lead to antibody diversity and heavy chain Ig class-switching. Postfollicular B-cells also demonstrate somatic Ig mutations, but not ongoing mutation. Literally any stage during B-cell differentiation can become neoplastic.

Lymph Nodes

Lymph nodes are small structures lying along the course of lymphatics. They are aggregated in particular sites such as the neck, axillae, groin and para-aortic region. Lymph nodes have two main functions:

- Phagocytic cells act as filters for particulate matter and micro-organisms
- Antigen is presented to the immune cells

Lymph nodes are essentially small connective tissue bags filled with mobile cells organized into functional compartments by a meshwork of reticular fibers, specialized blood vessels and nerve fibers. Two regions are recognized; an outer"cortex" and inner "medulla" that are distinguishable in histological sections by the relative density of small lymphoid cells.

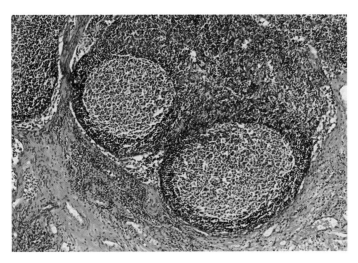

Figure 4.6 Reactive lymph node, H + E stain.

Cortex

B-cells enter lymph nodes, pass to the follicles, and if activated by antigenic stimulation, they proliferate and remain in the node (Figure 4.6). This is termed lymphoid hyperplasia. Unstimulated B cells, however, rapidly pass out of the node and return to the general circulation (recirculating B-cell pool). Activated B-cells within the follicles are known as follicle center cells. The pale staining central area of a secondary follicle is known as a germinal center and a mantle zone comprised of small, naive B cells and a few T cells surrounds this.

Stimulated mature B cells responding to antigen change into centrocytes and then centroblasts. The centroblasts leave the follicle and pass to the paracortex and medullary sinuses, where they become B-cell immunoblasts. The immunoblasts divide to give rise to plasma cells or memory B cells which are ready for their next encounter with specific antigen.

Lymphocytes alone do not make an effective immune response. They are assisted by so-called accessory cells including:

- Sinus macrophages (highly phagocytic)
- Tingible body macrophages (ingest cellular debris in germinal centers)
- Marginal zone macrophages (found beneath the subcapsular sinus)
- Follicular dendritic cells

Germinal Center B-Cells

Naïve, sIgM+ B-cells that recognize antigens with their sIg collect in the germinal centers of secondary lymphoid organs including lymph nodes, spleen, and mucosa-associated lymphoid tissue (MALT). The genomic DNA of the B cells may then be subjected to three types of modification:

- Somatic hypermutation
- Class switching
- Receptor editing

Somatic hypermutation is a process by which mutations are introduced at a high rate into V-region genes. As a result, some B-cell mutants in germinal centers produce antibodies with increased affinity for the immunizing antigen and are positively selected. Eventually, cells expressing favorable antibody mutants are released into the periphery as plasma cells or long-lived memory B cells. Many mutated germinal-center B cells, however, either lose the ability to bind antigen or fail to produce a functional antibody and undergo apoptotic cell death.

Finally, some B cells in germinal centers switch from expressing IgM and IgD to expressing heavy chains of other classes of immunoglobulin: IgG, IgA, or IgE. This results in a change in the effector functions of the antibody but leaves the V(D)J region (and consequently antibody specificity) unaltered. Class switching is mediated by a recombination event that deletes the DNA between repeated sequences (called switch regions) located upstream of the constant region of Ig heavy-chain genes.

Although the deep cortex is commonly known as the T-dependent cortex it is not comprised solely of T cells. The lymphocytes populating the deep cortex are about 75% T-cells and 25% B-cells, 90% of them are small lymphocytes and virtually all belong to the recirculating pool. Small B cells appear to migrate up to the superficial cortex after briefly accumulating around HEV. Small T cells move out through the perivenular channels into corridors of reticulum comprising the paracortex.

There are slightly more CD8+ T-cells compared with CD4+ T-cells in resting lymph nodes but the ratio can vary considerably. This also applies to the ratio of T cells to B-cells. After alloantigenic stimulation lymph nodes fill up with T-cells. In contrast, after inoculation of an antigen which selectively induces an antibody response, the deep cortex contains nearly 60% B-cells. Therefore, the deep cortex is a dynamic lymphatic compartment which responds to stimulation by cytokines, antigens, and other biological response modifiers.

Paracortex

The paracortex is the predominant site for T-cells within the lymph node. The various types of T-cell enter the node from the blood, and when activated, they form T-cell lymphoblasts which can divide to produce a clone of T-cells responding to a specific antigen. Activated T-cells pass into the circulation to reach peripheral sites. Interdigitating cells are numerous in the paracortex and they act as antigen-presenting cells (APC).

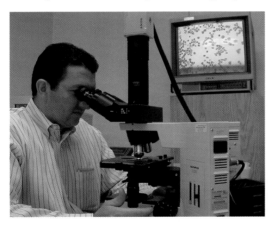

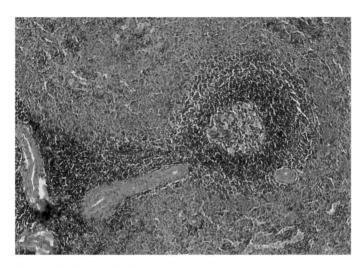

Figure 4.7 Spleen, H + E stain.>

Medulla

The medulla contains:

- Large blood vessels
- Medullary cords
- Medullary sinuses

The medullary cords are rich in plasma cells which produce antibodies that pass from the node via the efferent lymphatic. Macrophages are also numerous within the medulla.

The Spleen

The spleen is located in the upper left quadrant of the abdomen. It has two main functions acting as part of the immune system and as a filter.

The spleen filters blood and is the largest single lymphoid organ in the body. It receives a large proportion of the cardiac output, which contributes to its effectiveness as a filter of blood and a site for lymphocyte recirculation and lodging. Filtration of dead cells, debris and microorganisms occurs primarily in the reticulum of the red pulp chords and in the seive-like endothelium of venous sinuses. Reticular cells provide anchoring sites for mononuclear phagocytes that perform reticuloendothelial functions in the red pulp and marginal zone. The white pulp of the spleen contains a peripheral lymphatic tissue microenvironment for antigen trapping, cellular collaboration, lymphocyte proliferation and antibody production in addition to providing young bone marrow emigrant B-cells a place to complete maturation. The spleen is the primary site for initiation of immune responses to antigens and pathogens that have invaded the blood stream. Additionally, the spleen is a partner in every other immune response in the body. Antigen-laden mononuclear cells and lymphoblasts, released into efferent lymph from other lymphatic tissues, lodge in the spleen and set up satellite zones of T- and B-cell proliferation. During active immune responses immunoblastic B-cells committed to plasma cell differentiation lodge in the red pulp cords and sinuses where they mature and commence secreting antibody.

The marginal zone contains numerous B-cells which express membrane IgM+, IgD-, IL-2 receptors, have alkaline phosphatase on their surfaces and appear to be relatively sessile components of the marginal zone. The marginal zone IgM+, IgD- B-cells are post follicular IgM+, IgD+ cells. This population of B-cells appears to be enriched in those that selectively respond to type-2 thymus independent antigens while the follicular B-cells respond to thymic dependent antigens.

Mucosa-associated lymphoid tissue (MALT)

In addition to the lymphoid tissue concentrated within the lymph nodes and spleen, lymphoid tissue is also found at other sites, most notably the gastrointestinal tract, respiratory tract and urogenital tract.

This comprises:

- Tonsils, adenoids (Waldeyer's ring)
- Peyer's patches
- Diffusely distributed lymphoid cells and plasma cells in the lamina propria of the gut

Lymphocytic Traffic

During times of high lymphocyte production, a number of interesting quantitative and qualitative aspects of peripheral blood lymphocytosis come into play.

- Although virtually any type of lymphohematopoietic cell may be found in afferent lymph fluid flowing into the lymph nodes, only lymphocytes are found in exiting efferent lymph; the output from subcutaneous lymph nodes has been quantified at 30×10^6 cells/hour/gram of tissue.

- A single afferent lymphatic (of which 6-12 are usually associated with each lymph node) provides only 1×10^6 cells/hour to the node, or about 10% of the outflowing efferent content.

- Measurements of efferent lymph show that only 5% of cells were recently produced in the node, with the remainder coming from cells recently arrived from blood.

Not all lymphocyte subsets recirculate equally.

- Measurements of blood lymphocytes may not reflect the dynamic process of lymphocyte recirculation.

- Many of the B-cells in blood are naïve and making a one-way trip to lymph nodes; probably from the bone marrow.

- Cytokines and chemokines likely play a role in specific sequestration of lymphoid cells within lymph nodes (and other tissues).

- Certain cytokines, such as interferon gamma (INF-γ), interferon alpha (INF-α), and tumor necrosis factor alpha (TNF-α) have been shown to have an in vivo role in regulating lymphocyte traffic.

- INF-α regulates B-cell traffic within the germinal center, and may then serve to attract and selectively sequester CD21 (INF-α receptor)+ B-cells in germinal centers during immune responses.

The migration of resting and activated lymphocytes follow different patterns and have different characteristics.

- One major difference is the requirement for antigen by the activated cells, which undergo mitotic cell divisions, mainly in target organs.

- A second, related difference, is the life span of these cells. Resting lymphocytes are relatively long-lived, while activated cells have life spans measured in hours or a few days.

- The lymphocytes that continually recirculate between blood and lymph are small, high density cells.

- The large, low-density basophilic lymphocytes migrate to specific target organs or tissues, but do not traverse lymph.

- The continuous recirculation of lymphocytes is presumably related to immune surveillance, which seems separate from the job of activated lymphocytes.

Another difference between lymphocyte behavior in normal, as opposed to reactive lymph nodes, is the overall traffic pattern. In acute and chronic reactive lesions, there is a very high traffic of lymphoid cells on the order of 30-fold higher than in non-reactive lymph nodes.

In aggregate, the process of reactive lymphocytosis is complex, but capable of generating enormous numbers of lymphocytes. Thus, the dynamic process of production and removal dictate the pattern and number of lymphocyte subsets present in blood at any one snapshot in time.

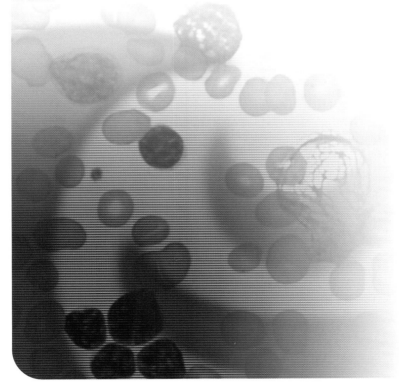

chapter **5**

Reactive Lymphoid Proliferations

A peripheral blood lymphocytosis, as mentioned earlier, can be either a benign, reactive lymphocytosis, or can be neoplastic as in NHL. When a peripheral lymphocytosis is first detected, usually by automated hematology analyzers, the next step in the process should be that of morphologic confirmation of the lymphocytosis and the inclusion of a morphologic interpretation in the context of a diagnosis, or of the next steps that should be taken in evaluation.

Role of Morphology

Morphologic examination of lymphocytosis may be strongly suggestive of certain reactive processes, or may instead lead to a diagnosis of certain lymphoid neoplasms. The following features, while helpful in determining the underlying cause, are not definitive in all cases, but are useful guidelines.

In the laboratory setting, a variety of terms have been used to describe non-malignant, reactive lymphocytes:

- Variant lymphocytes
- Atypical lymphocytes
- Reactive lymphocytes
- Transformed lymphocytes
- Activated lymphocytes
- Stress lymphocytes

Some morphologic clues that lymphocytes may be reactive are:

- Usually exist as a heterogeneous population
- Both large and small lymphocytes present
- Some cells contain cytoplasmic basophilia, others may lack basophlia
- Mixture of cells with dense nuclear chromatin and some with open chromatin
- The cytoplasm is frequently indented by surrounding RBC

Conversely, malignant lymphocytosis is suggested by:

- Cells more uniform in size
- Uniformity of nuclear chromatin pattern
- Uniformity in cytoplasmic features
- Frequently show cleaved or clefted nucleus

Clinical Information

The clinical history and the age of the patient, as well as the issue of relative versus absolute lymphocytosis, are useful in decision-making. A persistent lymphocytosis is more likely to be neoplastic, in that most reactive cases derive from infections that will be clinically evident, or of limited duration. Younger patients, particularly children, are less likely to have circulating lymphomas of mature cells than older adults. It must also be recognized that there are variations in reference ranges for absolute (and relative) peripheral blood lymphocyte levels according to age. Younger children have higher lymphocyte numbers than adults, and this must be factored into decisions about the impact of lymphocytosis.

Causes of Benign Lymphocytosis

Benign lymphocytosis above the age-adjusted normal range most commonly arise in the setting of acute viral illnesses including Epstein-Barr virus (EBV), cytomegalovirus (CMV), or hepatitis, but other causes are known as well.

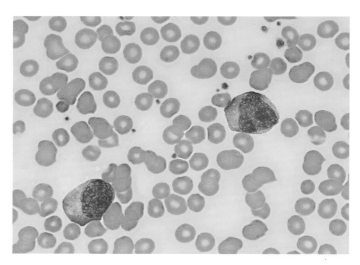

Figure 5.1 Peripheral Blood, EBV-positive infectious mononucleosis. Wright-Giemsa stain.

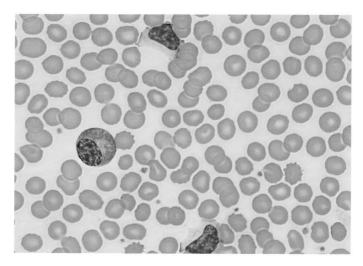

Figure 5.2 Peripheral Blood, acute Hepatitis C infection. Wright-Giemsa stain.

In the context of morphology, the group of infections that includes most viral illnesses usually elicits a reactive morphology (Figures 5.1 and 5.2).

- Heterogeneity of cells in size, shape, and nuclear features
- Cytoplasmic basophilia is common
- Cytoplasm frequently indented by surrounding red blood cells

On the other hand, there is a group of infectious agents that incites a lymphocytosis comprised of "non-reactive" morphology (Figure 5.3).

- Bordetella pertussis (mainly in children)
- Adenovirus
- Ehrlichia (during antibiotic treatment)
- Other non-specified viruses

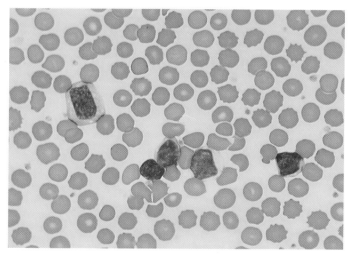

Figure 5.3 Peripheral Blood, Pertusis infection in child. Wright-Giemsa stain.

The morphology of these cells is typically similar to that of normal peripheral blood lymphocytes. In the case of Ehrlichiosis, the cells are of γ/δ T-cell type with mainly large granular lymphocyte morphology including cytoplasmic azurophilic granules.

Origins of Peripheral Blood Lymphocytosis

As stated earlier, the peripheral lymphoid tissues are capable of generating enormous numbers of lymphocytes. The overall immune system of humans comprises ~5 X 10^{11} lymphocytes, which continuously circulate in peripheral blood and lymphatics. The blood, however, contains only 2% of these cells, while the remaining 98% reside in lymphoid tissues. Thus, any small change in the entry, transit, and exit of lymphocytes from lymphoid tissues will have a significant effect on blood lymphocyte levels. As noted, lymph nodes are capable of expanding their production of lymphocytes by 30-fold during acute or chronic infections. The morphologic observations during these episodes are typically in the form of follicular hyperplasia (Figure 5.4).

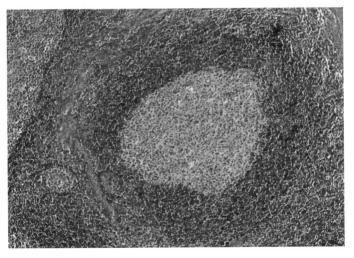

Figure 5.4 Reactive germinal center, tonsil. H + E stain.

Similarly, the spleen and other peripheral lymphoid tissues can undergo the same type of expansion to produce the cells that are needed to fight infections.

In the bone marrow, an acute lymphoid hyperplasia typically takes the form of increased production of hematogones (Figure 5.5). These small, compact lymphoid cells are predominantly B-cell precursors at various levels of maturation. Morphologically, they contain dense nuclear chromatin with indistinct nucleoli and have scant cytoplasm. The immunophenotypic spectrum of these cells involves at least 3 identifiable subsets:

- TdT+, bright CD10+, dim CD19+, with very dim CD45
- TdT+/-, dim CD10+, bright CD19+, with intermediate CD45
- The most mature subset is CD10-, CD19+, bright CD45, and expresses sIg

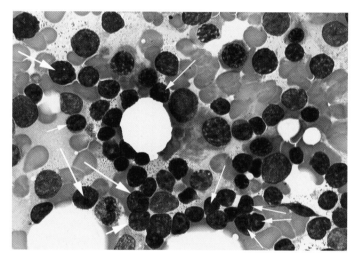

Figure 5.5 Bone marrow aspirate. Wright-Giemsa stain. The smaller arrows point to examples of subset 1 hematogones, while the larger arrows point to examples of subset 2 hematogones.

The smallest cells are those of subset 1, while the larger cells are subset 2, and subset 3 comprises normally sized lymphocytes. These cells can also be found in blood (Figure 5.6)

The bone marrow can also harbor manifestations of lymphoid reactions involving more mature cells. Typically, these take the form of either a diffuse increase in small lymphocytes, or more commonly, appear as lymphoid aggregates (Figures 5.7 and 5.8). While these aggregates do not likely contribute much to a peripheral blood lymphocytosis, their presence is likely to be an indicator that some pathologic process is ongoing. For instance, approximately 30% of elderly adults may have small numbers of lymphoid aggregates without peripheral blood lymphocytosis.

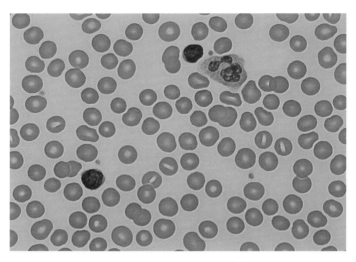

FIG 5.6 Peripheral Blood, child recovering from a recent unknown viral illness by clinical history. Wright-Giemsa stain.

Mostly, these aggregates are not associated with any specific disease entity or infection. However, in some cases lymphoid aggregates and/or granulomata are signs on infection. The main reason to consider lymphoid aggregates in our overview is because an unexplained peripheral lymphocytosis will sometimes trigger the performance of a bone marrow aspiration and biopsy. The differential diagnosis at this time becomes a benign reactive lymphocytosis versus small lymphoid lymphoma.

Morphologic features most commonly found in benign lymphoid aggregates include:

- Few in number
- Usually non-paratrabecular
- Well-circumscribed, usually round and discrete nodules
- Comprised of mature, polymorphous lymphocytes
- Occasionally, germinal centers are present
- Commonly perivascular

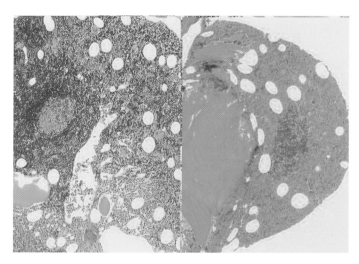

FIG 5.7 Bone marrow biopsies. The left panel shows a reactive lymphoid follicle, while the right side shows a small solitary lymphoid aggregate. H + E stain.

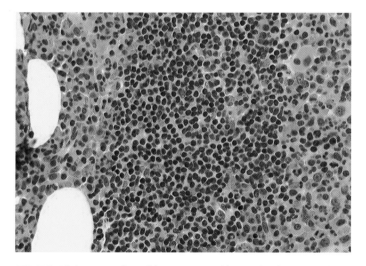

FIG 5.8 High-power view of bone marrow biopsy showing a small, well-circumscribed lymphoid aggregates. H + E stain.

Flow Cytometric Features of Reactive Hyperplasias

Obviously, the pattern of lymphocyte subsets circulating in the blood during processes that elicit lymphoid hyperplasia is dependent on the underlying cause.

For instance, in the common viral infections with EBV or CMV, a prominent lymphocytosis of CD8+/CD57+ cells is quite common, presumably this is a response to the infected B-cells. Some patienta with acute HIV will have a γ/δ T-cell lymphocytosis.

In the case of acute infection with Bordetella pertussis, the lymphocytosis is predominantly CD3+ T-cells, with the usual ratio of CD4:CD8 and percentage of B-cells. Reports indicate little immunophenotypic evidence of cellular activation, as evidenced by HLA-Dr-/CD3+.

In essentially all cases of reactive hyperplasias, the B-cell component demonstrates a polyclonal pattern, with both κ and λ light chains being expressed appropriately.

Summary

Many infectious and autoimmune processes may cause reactive lymphoid proliferations. However, the most common of these is underlying infection. The reaction in the bone marrow and peripheral lymphoid organs depends on the inciting agent. Overall, the process is characterized by morphologic and immunophenotypic heterogeneity and a polyclonal immune response.

chapter 6

Classification of Lymphoid Neoplasms

When considering a lymphocytosis to be secondary to the presence of lymphoid malignancies, consideration should be given to just what name to place on the disease. In many cases, the best information derived is simply that this is a clonal neoplastic disease that warrants further workup for a complete diagnosis. In other cases, it is possible to ascribe a likely diagnosis from peripheral blood alone. In these instances, the decision whether or not to pursue further bone marrow or soft tissue biopsies will depend on a number of clinical factors.

Nevertheless, it is important to have a good understanding of current classifications of lymphoma in order to employ the same terminology and to understand why a workup of peripheral blood should be more, or less, extensive at that point in time. If the clinician plans to obtain a lymph node biopsy, then the only important information from the blood is whether or not clonality is present. The complete evaluation should ideally be performed on the cells from the lymph node excisional biopsy. Occasionally, there are reasons why a biopsy cannot be performed right away; perhaps there are no discernable lymph nodes enlarged, or the enlarged lymph nodes are deep in the abdomen and require a surgical laparotomy. In such cases, it is better to supply more detailed information, if possible.

Classifications of lymphoid neoplasms have been an ever-evolving area of reassessment and refinement. This is mainly due to improvements in our understanding of this group of diseases.

The Revised European American Classification of Lymphoid Neoplasms

The Revised European American Classification of Lymphoid Neoplasms (REAL) evolved from an international effort that realized lymphoma was not a single disease, but rather multiple diseases, each with certain defining characteristics. The REAL group proposed that lymphomas could best be classified using a combination of information derived from morphology, immunophenotype, genetics, and clinical features. Further, they advocated classifying lymphomas on the basis of their putative normal counterpart of the neoplastic cells.

More detailed information, and the criteria for each class, are available in Blood 84:1361-1392, 1994. This publication was an important step in changing lymphoma classification to more clearly represent the evolving understanding and importance of molecular and biological characterization of the disease.

REAL Classification of Lymphoid Neoplasms

B Cell

- Precursor B-Cell Neoplasms
  - Pre-B-Cell Lymphoblastic Leukemia/Lymphoma
- Peripheral B-Cell Neoplasms
  - B-Cell CLL/Small Lymphocytic Lymphoma
  - Lymphoplasmacytoid Lymphoma/Immunocytoma
  - Mantle Cell Lymphoma
  - Follicle Center Lymphoma, Follicular
      Small Cell, Mixed Small- and Large-Cell, Large-Cell
      Diffuse, Predominantly Small-Cell
- Marginal Zone B-cell Lymphoma
  - Extranodal (MALT +/- monocytoid)
  - Nodal (+/- monocytoid)
  - Splenic (+/- villous)
- Hairy Cell Leukemia
- Plasmacytoma/myeloma

- Diffuse Large B-Cell
  - Primary Mediastinal B-Cell Subtype
- Burkitt's Lymphoma

T Cell

- Precursor T-Cell Neoplasms
  - T-cell lymphoblastic leukemia/lymphoma
- Peripheral T-Cell and NK-Cell Neoplasms
  - T-Cell CLL/Prolymphocytic
  - Large Granular Lymphocyte Leukemia (T-Cell and NK-Cell)
  - Mycosis Fungoides/Sezary Cell Leukmemia
  - Peripheral T-Cell Lymphoma
    Mixed Medium and Large-Cell, Large-Cell, Lymphoepithelioid
    Angioimmunoblastic T-Cell Lymphoma (AILD)
- Angiocentric Lymphoma
- Intestinal T-Cell Lymphoma (+/- enteropathy)
- Adult T-Cell Lymphoma/Leukemia (HTLV-1)
- Anaplastic Large-Cell Lymphoma (ALCL – CD30+),
  T and Null Cell

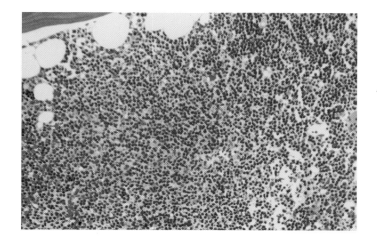

The World Health Organization Classification

The World Health Organization (WHO) has been a longstanding repository of books describing tumor classifications in pathology. The WHO classification of lymphoma and leukemia is now 25 years old. A newer version is now being put together by an international consensus group based largely on the REAL classification, but with certain refinements based on more recent and pertinent knowledge. A draft version of this proposed World Health Organization Classification of Neoplastic Diseases of the Hematopoietic and Lymphoid Tissues was made public in 1997, with further subsequent refinements. This document addresses not only lymphomas, but also other hematopoietic malignancies.

One important observation in the REAL classification, and emphasized in the WHO classification was that chronic lymphoid leukemias were actually more advanced stages of certain lymphomas, a relationship that was also observed in acute lymphoblastic leukemias and lymphoblastic lymphomas. Therefore, these lymphoid leukemias were reclassified along with the lymphomas.

Proposed WHO Classification of Lymphoid Neoplasms (February 1998)

B Cell Neoplasms

- Precursor B-Cell Neoplasm
  - Precursor-B-Cell Lymphoblastic Leukemia/Lymphoma

- Mature B-Cell Neoplasms
  - B-Cell Chronic Lymphocytic Leukemia/Small Lymphocytic Lymphoma
  - B-Cell Prolymphocytic Leukemia
  - Lymphoplasmacytic Lymphoma
  - Mantle Cell Lymphoma
  - Follicular Lymphoma
  - Marginal Zone B-cell Lymphoma of mucosa-associated lymphoid tissue (MALT) type
  - Nodal Marginal Zone B-cell Lymphoma (+/- Monocytoid B-Cells)

- Splenic Marginal Zone B-cell Lymphoma

- Hairy Cell Leukemia

- Diffuse Large B-Cell Lymphoma

> Subtypes: Mediastinal (Thymic), Intravascular, Primary Effusion Lymphoma
>
> Burkitt Lymphoma

- Plasmacytoma

- Plasma Cell Myeloma

T-Cell Neoplasms

- Precursor T-Cell Neoplasm

   - Precursor-T-Cell Lymphoblastic Leukemia/Lymphoma

- Mature T-Cell and NK-Cell Neoplasms

   - T-Cell Prolymphocytic Leukemia

   - T-Cell Granular Lymphocytic Leukemia

   - NK-Cell Leukemia

   - Extranodal NK/T-Cell Lymphoma, Nasal Type

   - Mycosis Fungoides

   - Sezary Syndrome

   - Angioimmunoblastic T-Cell Lymphoma

   - Peripheral T-Cell Lymphoma (Unspecified)

   - Adult T-Cell Lymphoma/Leukemia (HTLV1+)

   - Systemic Anaplastic Large-Cell Lymphoma (T and Null Cell Types)

   - Primary Cutaneous Anaplastic Large-Cell Lymphoma

   - Subcutaneous Panniculitis-Like T-Cell Lymphoma

   - Enteropathy-Type T-Cell Lymphoma

   - Hepatosplenic Gamma/Delta T-Cell Lymphoma

The above list only includes the non-Hodgkin lymphomas, although the complete WHO classification includes Hodgkin's lymphoma.

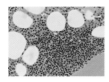

Differential Evaluation of Small Lymphoid Malignancies in Blood

Not all the lymphoid neoplasms listed in the WHO classification above commonly circulate in the blood, although in advanced stages of disease others can occasionally be found in blood. The vast majority of neoplastic lymphocytoses are those involving B-cells. The T-cell and NK-cell neoplasms are rare in occurrence. Precursor B- and T-lymphoblastic leukemia/lymphoma are the equivalent of acute leukemia or high grade lymphoma. Therefore, the most likely malignant lymphocytoses are found in the "mature B-Cell Neoplasms."

B Cell Neoplasms

- Precursor B-Cell Neoplasm
  - Precursor-B-Cell Lymphoblastic Leukemia/Lymphoma
- Mature B-Cell Neoplasms
  - B-Cell Chronic Lymphocytic Leukemia/Small Lymphocytic Lymphoma
  - B-Cell Prolymphocytic Leukemia
  - Lymphoplasmacytic Lymphoma
  - Mantle Cell Lymphoma
  - Follicular Lymphoma
  - Splenic Marginal Zone B-cell Lymphoma
  - Hairy Cell Leukemia
  - Burkitt Lymphoma

T-Cell Neoplasms

- Precursor T-Cell Neoplasm
  - Precursor-T-Cell Lymphoblastic Leukemia/Lymphoma

Mature T-Cell and NK-Cell Neoplasms

- T-Cell Prolymphocytic Leukemia
- T-Cell Granular Lymphocytic Leukemia
- NK-Cell Leukemia
- Sezary Syndrome
- Adult T-Cell Lymphoma/Leukemia (HTLV1+)

Certainly, the most common of these peripheral lymphocytoses is B-Cell CLL/SLL, but recently, the identification of mantle cell lymphoma (MCL) as a distinct entity has then altered this proportion, since some cases of MCL were likely previously diagnosed as B-Cell CLL/SLL. This is an important distinction, because MCL is a more aggressive disease and more difficult to treat successfully.

References

Harris N, et al. A revised European-American classification of lymphoid neoplasms: a proposal from the International Study Group. Blood 1995; 84:1361.

Harris, NL, et al: World Health Organization classification of neoplastic diseases of the hematopoietic and lymphoid tissues: report of the clinical advisory committee meeting – Airlie House, Virginia, November 1997. J Clin Oncol 17: 3835, 1999.

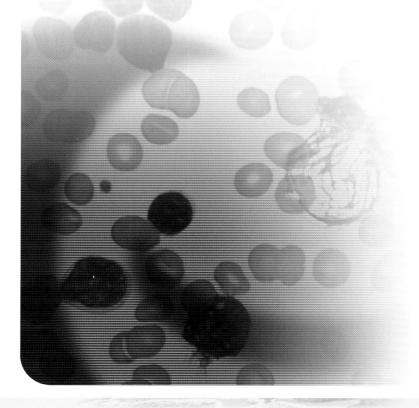

a p p e n d i x A

Lymphocytosis Cases and Reference Tables

his appendix contains a series of clinical laboratory cases that illustrate the approach to using automated hematology, microscopic morphology, and immunophenotyping by flow cytometry to examine the finding of peripheral blood lymphocytosis. These cases include pertinent background information about the disease entity under investigation, and specific observations that help discriminate between similar entities. Not every potential cause of lymphocytosis is included as a case presentation, but the cases selected are hopefully of interest and will elicit further reading and examination.

Following the clinical cases is a series of three tables that include pertinent information about the monoclonal antibodies that provide the foundation for immunophenotyping lymphocytoses. These are not entirely exhaustive, and some variation may occur between laboratories, as in the choice of multicolor conjugates, manufacturers, and composite panels. Whereas the examples included in this book utilize mainly the IoTest3 reagents from Beckman Coulter, similar results should be obtainable with other reagents.

Finally, the last two tables in this Appendix is a summary of the most common B-cell and T-cell lymphomas that circulate in the blood.

An Elderly Man With Decreased Activity and Bruising

An 87 year old man presented with decreased physical activity. In addition, he had several large bruises on both legs and arms. He also noticed a "lump under my arm". On physical examination, he was found to have multiple enlarged lymph nodes in his left axilla, and also a moderately enlarged spleen. A hematology profile was ordered as part of an examination for suspected lymphoma.

TABLE 1.1 – MAXM® Results

- WBC: 66.5 K/µL
- Platelets: 33 K/µL
- RBC: 2.82 M/µL
- RDW: 16.9 units
- Hemoglobin: 9.0 g/dL
- Hematocrit: 26%

Suspect flags: Blasts, Variant lymphs.

Definitive flags: Thrombocytopenia.

The WBC scatterplot obtained from a MAXM showed a predominant population of cells in the lymphocyte area (Figure 1.1). These cells were determined by morphologic review to be small lymphoid cells with agranular cytoplasm and rounded nuclei with mature nuclear chromatin clumping, occasional larger lymphoid cells with modest amounts of cytoplasm and a small nucleolus. Additionally present were numerous "smudge cells" (Figure 1.2). Since these cells have few granules, light scatter is reduced, accounting for the position on the left of the DF1 display (x=scatter, y=volume.

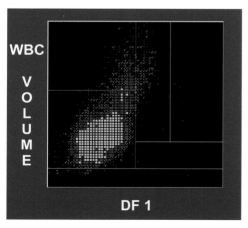

Figure 1.1 WBC scattergram from a MAXM.

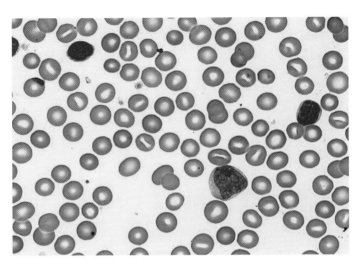

Figure 1.2 Peripheral Blood 1000x, Magnification Wright-Giemsa stain.

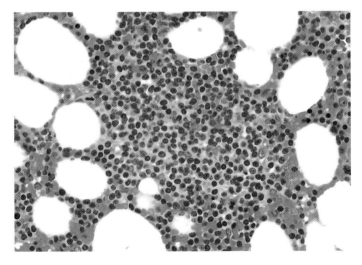

Figure 1.3 Bone Marrow Biopsy 400X, Magnification H+E stain.

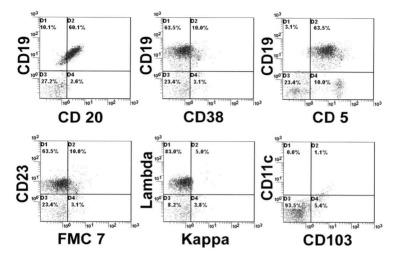

Figure 1.4 Representative historgrams from flow cytometry.

A flow cytometric examination of peripheral blood was ordered to further evaluate this lymphocytosis. Histograms and data from 3-color immunophenotyping are shown below.

The intensity of staining for CD20 is dimmer than that of CD19, with a CD19:CD20 ratio of >1. Very little CD38 is expressed on the CD19+ cells. CD5 is present on virtually all CD19+ cells. Of note, the intensity of CD5 on these B-cells is less than that of the CD19- T-cells. CD23 is also present, with only minimal expression of FMC7. Immunoglobulin light chain expression of lambda is present, and both CD11c and CD103 are negative. Thus, the reported immunophenotype of this lymphocytosis is: CD5+, CD19+, CD20 (dim)+, CD23+, with monoclonal lambda light chain expression.

B-Cell Chronic Lymphocytic Leukemia/Small Lymphocytic Lymphoma

Introduction

B-chronic lymphocytic leukemia/small lymphocytic lymphoma (B-CLL/SLL) is the most common leukemia in the western world, but much less prevalent in Asia and Africa. Approximately 7,000 new cases are reported in the U.S. each year. Though rare in people under 30 years old, it attains an incidence close to 50 per 100,000 after the age of 70. At the time of presentation, most patients will have blood and bone marrow involvement, with or without lymphadenopathy and hepatospenomegaly. Therefore, as a cause of lymphocytosis, this represents a fairly common finding in older individuals in the western world. Although an indolent disease, it is also a currently incurable neoplasm, with median survivals of >10 years for those presenting with low stage disease. Prognosis is stage dependent, and is often strongly correlated with doubling time of the blood lymphocytes. Other adverse features include prolymphocytoid morphology, trisomy 12, deletion of chromosome 17p and p53 gene mutations. More common cytogenetic abnormalities (deletion of 13q14 and 11q22-23) do not correlate with more aggressive disease. Approximately 5% of cases will transform into an aggressive large cell lymphoma called the Richter's transformation.

A familial tendency has also been documented with the intriguing phenomenon of anticipation: families in which B-CLL/SLL appears in succeeding generations at an ever-earlier age. The disease has a prolonged natural history, sometimes measured in decades, and gradually acquires sequential genetic abnormalities rendering it even more malignant.

Not all cases of B CLL/SLL are indolent, even when corrected for stage. As such, there has been a great deal of interest in trying to define those cases which act more aggressively. This has included cytogenetic, nucleic acid and immunophenotypic analysis, along with morphology and advancement of stage. Several groups have found that white blood cell count (WBC), lymphocyte doubling times and Binet clinical stages have been proven to be the most prognostic markers in multivariant studies.

The malignant cell in B-CLL/SLL is a small, fragile B lymphocyte whose immunophenotype resembles that of lymphocytes in the mantle zone (MZ) of secondary lymphoid follicles. The most distinctive feature of B-CLL/SLL cells is the co-expression of CD5 with CD19 and CD20 with very faint amounts of monoclonal sIg; usually IgM ± IgD and rarely IgG or IgA. Surface levels of IgM as low as in B-CLL/SLL are seen only in normal B cells that have been anergized by interaction with self antigen (Ag).

One potential influence on the development of lymphoid malignancies is exerted by the Ag encounter that occurs in germinal centers (GC) of the secondary lymphoid follicles and leads to the process of Ig somatic muta-tion. Point mutations are introduced into Ig-V-gene sequences and result in the production of antibodies with high affinity. The examination of Ig-V gene sequences in B-CLL/SLL has revealed the presence of somatic muta-tions in approximately half the cases. This finding implies that the cell of origin in these cases is a memory B cell that has passed through an Ag experience in germinal centers of secondary follicles. The other B-CLL/SLL cases show no mutations, indicating that they originate from naive B cells that have no Ag experience.

It has also been shown that B-CLL/SLL with unmutated Ig-V genes have much higher percentages of CD38-positive cells. This has clinical rele-vance, as the prognosis of B-CLL/SLL arising from naive B cells appears to be worse than the prognosis of B-CLL/SLL arising from memory B cells. Thus an immunophenotypic subclassification that relates to molecular genetic alterations and clinical outcomes helps explain the heterogeneity in natural history of this disease. Furthermore, it may help identify patients requiring no treatment and others that need intensive therapy.

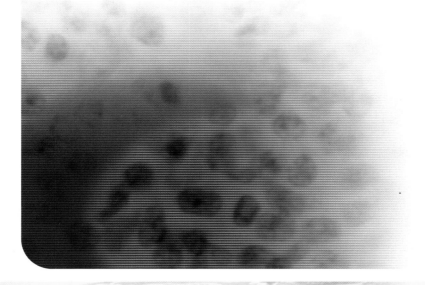

Clinical Features

History:

B-CLL/SLL is usually insidious in onset, and is indolent, but not currently curable. It is not unusual for this disorder to be discovered incidentally on a routine blood count done for another reason. Most all cases of B-CLL/SLL are associated with peripheral blood involvement. Other salient features include:

- Predisposition to repeated infections like pneumonia, herpes simplex, herpes zoster, etc.
- Early satiety and/or abdominal discomfort related to an enlarged spleen
- Bleeding from mucous surfaces and/or petechiae or bruises from thrombocytopenia
- Tiredness/fatigue from anemia

Physical Exam:

- Localized or generalized lymphadenopathy
- Splenomegaly (30 to 40% of cases)
- Hepatomegaly (20% of cases)
- Petechiae
- Pallor

Complications:

- Hypogammaglobinemia and decreased T-cell function predisposes patients to infections. Patients who demonstrate a pattern of repeated infections, such a pneumonia and septicemia, may benefit from IV infusions of IgG.
- Anemia secondary to bone marrow involvement with B-CLL/SLL, splenic sequestration of RBCs, and Coomb's-positive autoimmune hemolytic anemia are included in the differential diagnosis of anemia in B-CLL/SLL.
- Thrombocytopenia; causes in B-CLL/SLL are similar to those of anemia in CLL and include bone marrow involvement, splenic sequestration, and immune thrombocytopenia.

Laboratory Workup

- Complete blood count with differential shows absolute lymphocytosis, usually with >5000 lymphocytes/mm3.

- Peripheral blood smear confirms lymphocytosis and usually shows the presence of smudge cells, which are artifacts due to broken lymphocytes during the slide preparation.

- Serum quantitative Ig levels in patients with repeated infections since monthly intravenous Ig administration in these patients reduces the frequency of infections.

- Bone marrow aspiration/biopsy is not required in all cases, but may be necessary in selected cases to establish the diagnosis as well as to assess other complicating features such as thrombocytopenia.

- Lymph node biopsy if node(s) rapidly enlarge. This will assess the possibility of transformation to a high grade lymphoma, such as Richter's syndrome.

Morphology

Peripheral blood B-CLL/SLL cells are small lymphocytes with modest amounts of pale basophilic cytoplasm and nuclei with usually round contours and mature or "blocky" chromatin clumping with or without a small nucleolus. In general, these are slightly larger than normal lymphocytes. However, large cells with more abundant cytoplasm suggests a differential diagnosis including all circulating lymphomas of mature maturation.

Immunophenotype / Differential Diagnosis

The differential diagnosis of B-CLL/SLL is primarily with the leukemic phase of mantle cell lymphoma (MCL) and plasmacytoid SLLs. The leukemic phase of a marginal zone lymphoma (MZL) is distinctly less common that B-CLL/SLL. The flow cytometric immunophenotypic differentiation begins with CD5, CD10, and CD23 expression. The CD5+ / CD10- / CD23+ profile in a mature monoclonal B lymphocytosis is virtually diagnostic of B-CLL/SLL.

- Peripheral blood flow cytometry is the most valuable test to confirm B-CLL/SLL. It confirms the presence of circulating clonal B-lymphocytes expressing CD5, CD19, CD20, CD 23(dim), and an absence of FMC-7 staining.

- The typical immunophenotype of B-CLL/SLL cells is that of a monoclonal B-cell population expressing CD5, CD19/CD20, and CD23. They are usually negative for CD10 and CD79b, but may be weakly positive for FMC-7 and CD22.

- CD5 positivity usually indicates B-CLL/SLL or MCL, while CD23 positivity typically excludes MCL.

- CD38 may stratify patients with B-CLL/SLL into 2 clinically important groups; those with a slower, more benign course, and those with more rapidly progressive disease.

- Approximately 2-5% of CLL/SLL cases will have a T-cell immunophenotype.

- B-CLL/SLL typically shows a distinct profile clearly expressing CD5, CD21, CD23 and CD43 antigens, while lacking CD10 and CD103

Typically, B CLL/SLL is brightly CD45 positive, although it may show somewhat diminished fluorescence intensity compared to benign lymphocytes or other types of mature B lymphoid neoplasms.

B CLL/SLL is relatively unique among the mature lymphocytic leukemias/lymphomas, in that the density of surface immunoglobulin (sIg) is usually low or "dim". When detectable, the sIg has an IgM and/or IgD isotype.

The CD20 antigen is down-regulated on the cell surface, consistently "dimmer" than seen on normal B or other mature neoplastic B and creates an additional indicator or diagnosis. Since CD19 is not down-regulated, the ratio of the % CD19:CD20 positive cells is >1 in most cases, whereas the reverse is true of other B-cell neoplasms.

The presence of the CD38 antigen (> 30%+ B CLL cells) may be associated with a poor prognosis and germline DNA sequence for the variable segment of the Ig gene. The latter is also associated with poorer prognosis for B CLL.

Genetics

Molecular methods such as fluorescence in-situ hybridization (FISH), indicate as many as 80% of cases have clonal aberrations, the most common involves deletions at 13q. Patients with 13q14 abnormalities have stable or slowly progressive disease, show heavy somatic mutations of Ig genes, and lack CD38. Conversely, trisomy 12 correlates with so-called "atypical" morphology, unmutated VH genes, CD38 expression and progressive disease. p53 mutations, occurring in approximately 15% of cases, also correlate with poor prognosis and prolymphocytoid transformation.

Pearls of Immunophenotyping B-CLL/SLL:

Pearl 1: The malignant lymphocytes in B-CLL/SLL are B-cells, but they express CD5 which is a T cell marker. So does mantle cell lymphoma (MCL).

Pearl 2: B-CLL/SLL expresses CD23, MCL does not.

Pearl 3: The surface Ig staining in B-CLL/SLL is very dim, sometimes negative.

Pearl 4: The ratio of % positive CD19:CD20 is almost always >1 because CD20 is downregulated on the cells of B-CLL/SLL.

Pearl 5: The histogram of CD45 in B-CLL/SLL may show a dim peak, compared to normal T or B cells.

Pearl 6: Expression of CD38 is important to help stratify patients in low- or high-risk disease

References

Caligaris-Cappio F, Hamblin TJ: B-cell chronic lymphocytic leukemia: a bird of a different feather. J Clin Oncol 17:399. 1999

Fais F, Ghiotto F, Hashimoto S. et al: Chronic lymphocytic leukemia B cells express restricted sets of mutated and unmutated antigen receptors. J Clin Invest 102:1515. 1998

Hamblin TJ, Davis Z, Gardiner A, Oscier DG, Stevenson FK: Unmutated immunoglobolin V, genes are associated with a more aggressive form of chronic lymphocytic leukemia. Blood 94:1848, 1999

Damle RN, Wasill T, Fais F, et al: Immunoglobulin V gene mutation status and CD38 expression as novel prognostic indicators in chronic lymphocytic leukemia. Blood 94:1840, 1999

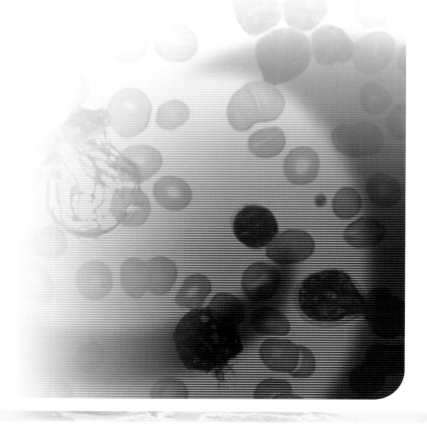

Man With a Swollen Lymph Gland

Case Presentation

A 55 year old man visited his primary care physician after he noticed a "swollen lymph gland" on the left side of his neck. He also said that when shaving, it seemed to take a long time to quit bleeding after nicking himself with a razor. On physical examination, he appeared pale and was found to have not only the enlarged lymph node he reported, but also multiple enlarged lymph nodes in both his axillae.

The hematology profile that was ordered resulted in a phone call from the laboratory stating that his WBC was over 600,000, his hemoglobin was 8.0 g/dL, and his platelet count was 8,000.

The WBC histogram from the MAXM® revealed a bizarre pattern of cells that created a continuum in the DF 1 display from the lymphoid region on up into the usual myeloid region (Figure 2.1).

Upon a manual slide review (Figure 2.2), the combination of low RBCs and markedly increased lymphoid cells was striking. There were certainly small, compact lymphocytes present, but also intermediate and larger lymphoid cells with prominent nucleoli.

TABLE 2.1 – MAXM® Results
• WBC: 606 K/µL
• Platelets: 8 K/µL
• RBC: 2.72 M/µL
• RDW: 15.9 units
• Hemoglobin: 8.0 g/dL
• Hematocrit: 26%
Suspect flags: Blasts, Variant lymphs.
Definitive flags: Thrombocytopenia.

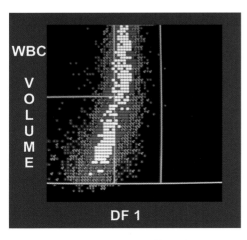

Figure 2.1 Automated WBC differential from MAXM.

casetwo

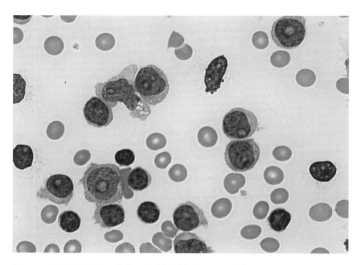

Figure 2.2 Peripheral Blood, Wright-Giemsa stain.

A microcentrifuged blood sample illustrated the dramatic relationship between RBC and WBC (Figure 2.3).

A bone marrow was the performed. The bone marrow biopsy showed an infiltrate with a diffuse pattern of small and intermediate-sized lymphocytes with occasional pale single histiocytes scattered throughout (Figure 2.3).

A lymphnode biopsy showed a predominantly mantle zone pattern with residual reactive germinal centers (Figure 2.4)

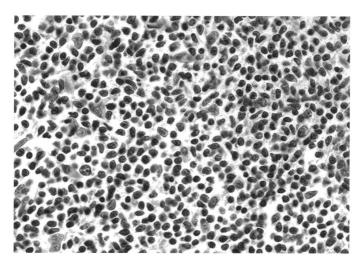

Figure 2.3 Bone Marrow Biopsy, H+E stain.

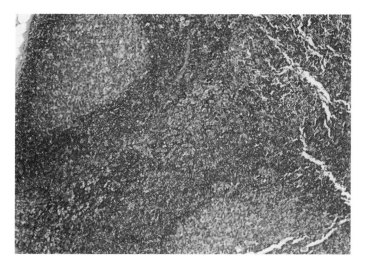

Figure 2.4 Lymph Node Biopsy, H+E stain.

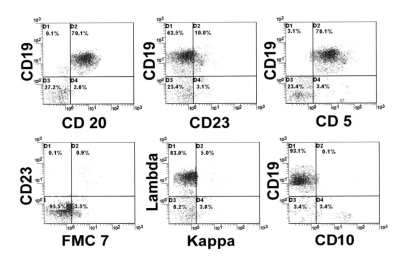

Figure 2.5 A flow cytometric examination of peripheral blood was ordered to further evaluate this lymphocytosis. Pertinent histograms and data from 3-color immunophenotyping are shown.

The intensity of staining for CD20 and that of CD19 are similar, with a CD19:CD20 percent positive ratio of ~1. CD5 is present on virtually all CD19+ cells. Of note, the intensity of CD5 on these B-cells is less than that of the CD19- T-cells. CD23 is absent, with only minimal expression of FMC7. Immunoglobulin light chain expression of lambda is present, and both CD11c and CD103 are negative. Thus, the reported immunophenotype of this lymphocytosis is: CD5+, CD19+, CD20+, CD23-, CD10-, with monoclonal lambda light chain expression.

Mantle Cell Lymphoma

Introduction

Mantle cell lymphoma (MCL), which comprises roughly 5-10% of non-Hodgkin's lymphomas in the United States and Europe, has only recently been formally defined as a distinct clinicopathologic entity. MCL is characterized by expansion of the mantle area of the lymph node by neoplastic small- to intermediate-sized lymphocytes typically with irregular nuclei, inconspicuous nucleoli, scant to moderate cytoplasm, an absence of proliferation centers, and unique immunologic and molecular features. The cells usually express bright sIg, CD5, CD19, CD20, and CD22, but lack expression of CD10 and CD23. Patients commonly present with advanced stage disease and undergo an aggressive clinical course. None of the available conventional chemotherapy regimens appears curative; hence, consideration of innovative treatment protocols and early bone marrow or stem cell transplantation appear warranted. MCL is now considered a distinct entity in both the Revised European American Lymphoma (REAL) and the World Health Organization (WHO) classification schemes and combines the previously recognized entities intermediate lymphocytic lymphoma, lymphocytic lymphoma of intermediate differentiation, centrocytic lymphoma, and mantle zone lymphoma. MCL can, but rarely presents as the blastic variant in the leukemic phase.

Clinical Features

History:

MCL has a wide range of symptoms and signs at presentation, but is not as insidious in onset as B-CLL/SLL. This disease is more aggressive and not currently considered curable. Many cases of MCL are associated with peripheral blood involvement, but not all cases. Other salient features are similar to B-CLL/SLL and include:

- Most common in in males over the age of 50
- Predisposition to repeated infections
- Abdominal discomfort related to an enlarged spleen
- Bleeding from mucous surfaces and/or petechiae or bruises from thrombocytopenia
- Tiredness/fatigue from anemia

Physical:

- Localized or generalized lymphadenopathy
- Splenomegaly (30 to 40% of cases)
- Hepatomegaly (20% of cases)
- Petechiae
- Pallor

Complications:

- Typically presents with disseminated involvement of multiple lymph node groups and infiltration of the bone marrow
- Usually more advanced stage of disease at diagnosis
- Extranondal disease is common
- Hepatosplenomegaly and lymphocytosis are common, and may present a clinical picture mimicking chronic lymphocytic leukemia

Laboratory Workup

- Complete blood count with differential shows absolute lymphocytosis, usually with markedly elevated absolute lymphocyte counts.
- Microscopic examination of peripheral blood smear confirms lymphocytosis and usually shows significant morphologic heterogeneity in size, shape and nuclear features.
- Bone marrow aspiration/biopsy is not required in all cases, but may be necessary in selected cases to establish the diagnosis as well as to assess other complicating features such as the differential diagnosis of thrombocytopenia (destruction versus hypoproduction).
- Lymph node biopsy is required for diagnostic histopathology.

Morphology

The peripheral blood MCL cells are typically of small-to-medium size with irregularly-shaped nuclei, small nucleoli and modest amounts of cytoplasm. They can be quite variable morphologically, ranging from small lymphocytes with modest amounts of pale basophilic cytoplasm and nuclei with round contours and mature or "blocky" chromatin, to also include, as in this case, larger cells with more abundant cytoplasm and nuclear heterogeneity including prominent nucleoli. In general, the MCL cells are larger than normal lymphocytes.

The leukemic morphology of the blastic variant of MCL is quite variable, ranging from mature lymphocytes to cells resembling prolymphocytes or even acute leukemic blasts. The cells are of intermediate size, with a high N/C ratio, mildly irregular nuclei and a finely dispersed nuclear chromatin without obvious nucleoli.

Bone marrow involvement is typical and the pattern can be nodular, interstitial, or diffuse. The core biopsy sections show cytology similar to classic MCL with small lymphocytes and occasional blast-like cells. Marrow aspirates nicely demonstrate the morphologic features.

Immunophenotype / Differential Diagnosis

The diagnosis of MCL may be strongly suspected from the initial morphologic review. However, given the aggressive behavior of this disease, additional immunophenotyping and/or genotyping along with histology should be used to make the definitive diagnosis.

- The most common immunophenotype of MCL includes positivity for: CD5, CD19, CD20, CD22, sIgM and sIgD (D > M/D; lambda > kappa). Of importance, they are usually CD23-, and negative for CD10.

- The immunophenotypic differential diagnosis of MCL includes all small lymphoid neoplasms of B-cell type, but mainly the problem is separating MCL from B-CLL/SLL

- CD5 positivity usually indicates B-CLL/SLL or MCL, while CD23 positivity typically excludes MCL.

- The intensity of staining of also of importance. CD20 staining is brighter in MCL than on B-CLL/SLL , as is staining for sIg.

- Hairy cell leukemia can be usually be eliminated by the lack of CD11c, CD103, and usually CD25.

Genetics

MCL is characterized by a t[11:14] translocation, which involves the bcl-1 (cyclin D1) and IgH genes. This translocation is detected in approximately two-thirds of patients by standard karyotyping, and in virtually all cases by fluorescence in situ hybridization (FISH). Although this is fairly specific for MCL, it has also been reported in unusual cases of B CLL/SLL, multiple myeloma, and approximately one third of B-cell prolymphocytic leukemias (B-PLLs).

Pearls of Immunophenotyping MCL:

Pearl 1: The malignant lymphocytes are B-cells expressing CD5. So does B-CLL/SLL.

Pearl 2: B-CLL/SLL expresses CD23, MCL does not.

Pearl 3: The surface Ig staining in MCL is brighter than B-CLL/SLL.

Pearl 4: The ratio of % positive CD19:CD20 is almost always ~1 because CD20 is not downregulated as in B-CLL/SLL.

Pearl 5: Cyclin D1 overexpression is a useful tool to help delineate MCL, as is cytogenetics for t[11:14].

References

Singleton TP, Anderson MM, Ross CW et al. Leukemic Phase of Mantle Cell Lymphoma, blastoid variant. Am J Clin Pathol 1999; 111:pp.495-500

Jaffe ES, Harris NL, Diebold J et al. World Health Organization Classification of Neoplastic Diseases of the Hematopoietic and Lymphoid tissues A Progress Report. Am J Clin Pathol 1999; 111 (Suppl.1):pp. S8-S12

Harris NL, Jaffe ES, Stein H et al: A revised European-American classification of lymphoid neoplasms: A proposal from the international lymphoma study group. Blood 84: 1361-1392, 1994.

Zucca E, Stein H, Coiffier B et al. European Lymphoma Task Force (ELTF): Report of the workshop on mantle cell lymphoma. Ann Oncol. 5: 507-511, 1994.

Woman With a Mass Found During Breast Exam

Case Presentation

A 48 year old woman noticed an enlargement under her left arm during a self-examination of her breasts. She did not make an appointment right away, thinking it might go away. Approximately 2 months later, it was still present and she made an appointment with her physician. On physical examination, she was found to have only the enlarged lymph node she reported. The node was approximately 2 cm in diameter. Although not certain, it was jointly decided the best course of action would be to have the node excised. As part of her pre-operative process, a hematology profile and coagulation studies were ordered.

The hematology profile showed a mild lymphocytosis with some "atypical" lymphocytes. The slide was reviewed by the pathologist, who expressed concerns of this being reactive versus neoplastic. Thus, additional flow cytometric studies were requested to answer this question.

The WBC histogram from the MAXM® revealed a pattern of cells in the DF 1 display that suggested an atypical population in the lymphoid region (Figure 3.1). Upon a manual slide review (Figure 3.2), there were mainly small, compact lymphocytes present, but also

TABLE 3.1 – MAXM® Results

- WBC: 10.1 K/µL
- Platelets: 270 K/µL
- RBC: 4.03 M/µL
- RDW: 9.9 units
- Hemoglobin: 14.2 g/dL
- Hematocrit: 42 %

Suspect flags: Variant lymphs.

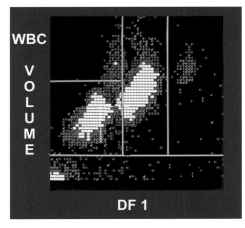

Figure 3.1 WBC scattergram from MAXM.

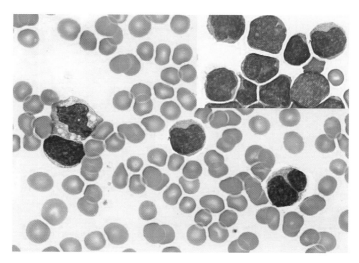

Figure 3.2 Peripheral Blood, Wright-Giemsa stain.

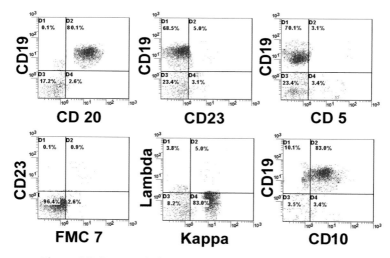

Figure 3.3 Representative histograms from 3-color analysis.

intermediate-sized lymphoid cells with somewhat cleaved nuclei, with occasional binucleate cells.

A flow cytometric examination of peripheral blood was ordered to further evaluate this lymphocytosis. Histograms and data from 3-color immunophenotyping gated on CD19+ B-cells are shown in Figure 3.3.

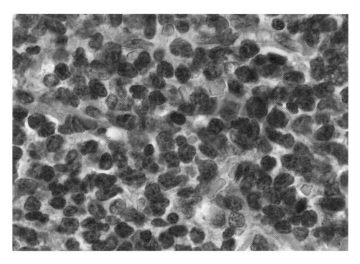

Figure 3.4 Bone Marrow Biopsy, H+E stain.

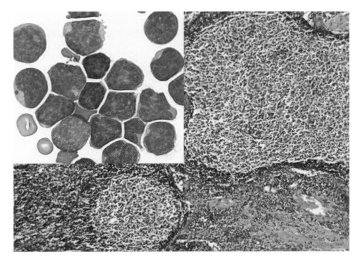

Figure 3.5 Lymph Node Biopsy, H+E stain. Note the follicular pattern and the morphology of the lymph node cell suspension after cytocentrifugation.

The intensity of staining for CD20 and that of CD19 are similar, with a CD19:CD20 percent-positive ratio of 1. CD10 is dimly expressed on most CD19+ cells. CD5, CD23, and FMC7 are absent. Immunoglobulin light chain expression of kappa is present. The reported immunophenotype of this lymphocytosis is: CD5-, CD19+, CD20+, CD23-, CD10+, with monoclonal kappa light chain expression.

On the basis of these findings, a bone marrow (Figure 3.4) and a lymph node biopsy were performed (Figure 3.5).

Since the follicular pattern by histology was so characteristic, and the flow cytometric data supported the diagnosis, no repeat immunophenotyping studies were performed on this tissue or the bone marrow.

Follicular Lymphoma

Introduction

Follicular lymphoma (FL), previously named follicle center lymphoma in the Revised European American Lymphoma (REAL), has been renamed in the World Health Organization (WHO) classification scheme. FL is a common form of non-Hodgkin's lymphoma in the United States and Europe, and is characterized by a follicular or nodular pattern comprised of neoplastic small- to intermediate-sized lymphocytes typically with cleaved or angulated nuclei, scant cytoplasm, and sometimes an absence of a mantle zone. Patients commonly present with advanced stage disease, but undergo relatively indolent clinical course. The 5 year survival is approximately 72%, making this one of the least aggressive lymphomas. Although none of the available conventional chemotherapy regimens currently appears curative, FL patients are showing an improvement in survival with more recent treatment regimens. FL can present in a leukemic phase, but this is generally a manifestation of an advanced stage of the disease.

Clinical Features

History:
FL typically presents with lymphadenopathy. Many, but not all cases of FL, are associated with peripheral blood involvement. Other salient features include:

- Most common in adults
- Median age 59 years
- Equal male:female ratio
- Tiredness/fatigue from anemia

Physical:

- Localized or generalized lymphadenopathy
- Thirty-three percent have early stage I-II disease
- Splenomegaly, and/or Hepatomegaly can occur advanced disease
- Bone marrow is commonly involved (42%)
- Uncommonly involves extranodal sites such as skin and GI tract

Complications:

- Hepatosplenomegaly and lymphocytosis are common, and may present a clinical picture mimicking splenic lymphomas

Laboratory Workup

- Complete blood count with differential may show an absolute lymphocytosis.
- Microscopic examination of peripheral blood smear usually shows morphologic heterogeneity in size, shape and nuclear features.
- Bone marrow aspiration/biopsy should be performed to determine the extent of disease.
- Lymph node biopsy is required for diagnostic histopathology.

Morphology

The peripheral blood FL cells are typically of small-to-medium size with irregularly-shaped cleaved or angulated nuclei, indistinct nucleoli and modest amounts of cytoplasm. In general, the FL cells are a little larger than normal lymphocytes.

Bone marrow involvement typically takes the form of paratrabecular lymphoid aggregates, but may also be diffusely replaced in advanced stages. Marrow aspirates nicely demonstrate the cleaved or angulated nuclear features.

Lymph node biopsies demonstrate a nodular of follicular pattern of lymphoma that may resemble non-malignant reactive lymphoid hyperplasia, thus the need for flow cytometry.

Immunophenotype / Differential Diagnosis

The diagnosis of FL may be strongly suspected from the initial morphologic review when a lymphocytosis is present with characteristic small cleaved lymphocytes. However, additional immunophenotyping should be used to make the definitive determination that these are indeed monoclonal B-cells when the lymphocyte count is increased in the apparent absence of enlarged lymph nodes. Most of the time, leukemic involvement is accompanied by significant nodal involvement.

- The most common immunophenotype of FL includes positivity for the B-cell antigens CD19, CD20, CD22, and sIg (M>G>A with or without sIgD).
- Most cases express (sometimes dimly) CD10.
- FL cells are CD5-, CD11c-, CD103-, and usually CD23-.
- The FL cells are immunophenotypically distinct from MCL and B-CLL/SLL with absent CD5.
- CD20 staining is brighter on FL than on B-CLL/SLL , as is staining for sIg.
- Co-expression of bcl-2 and CD20 is a good indicator of FL.
- Hairy cell leukemia can be usually be eliminated by the lack of CD11c, CD103, and usually CD25.

Genetics

FL is commonly associated with a t[14:18] translocation, which involves the bcl-2 gene that causes expression of an "anti-apoptosis" gene which is normally switched off at a translational level in follicle center cells. Both Ig heavy and light chain genes are clonally rearranged. The cells also demonstrate a high level of somatic mutations and intraclonal variation similar to ongoing mutations observed in non-neoplastic follicle center cells.

Pearls of Immunophenotyping FL:

Pearl 1: The malignant lymphocytes are B-cells expressing CD19 and CD20 equally.

Pearl 2: FL cells frequently express CD10, whereas most other mature B-cell lymphomas do not.

Pearl 3: The surface Ig staining in FL is brighter than B-CLL/SLL.

Pearl 4: Expression of bcl-2 is a useful tool to help delineate FL, as is cytogenetics for t[14:18].

References

Swerdlow SH: Small B-cell lymphomas of the lymph nodes and spleen: Practical insights to diagnosis and pathogenesis. Mod Pathol 12:125-140, 1998.

Jaffe ES, Harris NL, Diebold J et al. World Health Organization Classification of Neoplastic Diseases of the Hematopoietic and Lymphoid tissues A Progress Report. Am J Clin Pathol 1999; 111 (Suppl.1):pp. S8-S12

Harris NL, Jaffe ES, Stein H et al: A revised European-American classification of lymphoid neoplasms: A proposal from the international lymphoma study group. Blood 84: 1361-1392, 1994.

case four

Routine Physical Examination

Case Presentation

A 57 year old man was visiting his primary care physician for a long over-due physical examination. He claimed to be feeling just fine, and had really been quite healthy for years; his excuse for not having a recent exam. On physical examination, he did in fact appear to be in good physical shape for his age, but had a palpable spleen.

As part of his examination, his physician ordered a lipid chemistry panel and a hematology profile.

The WBC histogram from the MAXM® revealed a pattern of cells in the DF 1 display that showed a dual population in the lymphoid region (Figure 4.1). Upon a manual slide review (Figure 4.2), there was a mixture of small, compact lymphocytes and intermediate-sized lymphoid cells with more abundant cytoplasm, and mainly round to oval nuclei with visible nucleoli.

TABLE 4.1 – MAXM® Results

- WBC: 38.1 K/µL
- Platelets: 140 K/µL
- RBC: 5.03 M/µL
- RDW: 12.9 units
- Hemoglobin: 14.0 g/dL
- Hematocrit: 42 %

Suspect flags: Variant lymphs.

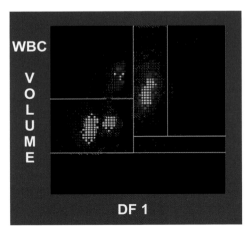

Figure 4.1 Automated WBC histogram from a MAXM.

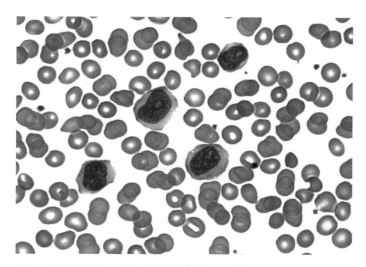

Figure 4.2 Peripheral Blood, Wright-Giemsa stain.

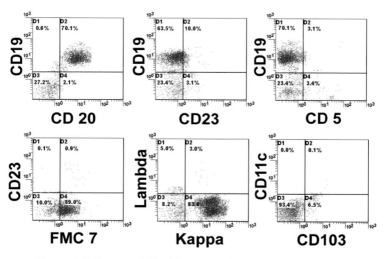

Figure 4.3 Representative histograms from 3-color analysis.

A flow cytometric examination of peripheral blood was ordered to further evaluate this lymphocytosis. Pertinent histograms and data from 3-color immunophenotyping gated on CD19+ B-cells are shown in Figure 4.3.

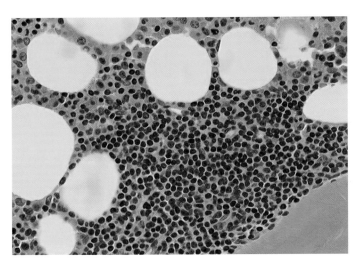

Figure 4.4 Bone Marrow Biopsy, H+E stain. Note the minimal involvement in a paratrabecular pattern.

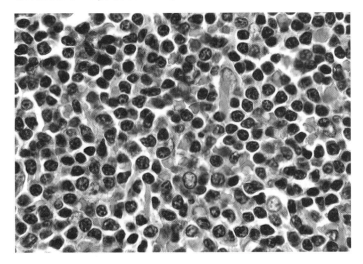

Figure 4.5 Spleen section, H+E stain.

CD20 and CD19 are similar in their positivity, with a CD19:CD20 percent-positive ratio of 1. FMC7 is dimly expressed on most CD19+ cells. CD5 and CD23 are absent, as well as CD11c and CD103. Immunoglobulin light chain expression of kappa is present. The reported immunophenotype of this lymphocytosis is: CD5-, CD19+, CD20+, CD23-, FMC7+, with monoclonal kappa light chain expression.

On the basis of these findings, and concern of a primary lymphoma of the spleen, a splenectomy was performed (Figure 4.4) with a bone marrow for staining (Figure 4.5). Since the marginal zone pattern by histology was characteristic, and the flow cytometric data supported the diagnosis, no repeat studies were performed on this tissue.

Splenic Marginal Zone B-Cell Lymphoma

Introduction

Splenic marginal zone B-cell lymphoma (MZBCL) was described in the Revised European American Lymphoma (REAL) classification, and is described in more detail in the World Health Organization (WHO) classification system. Splenic MZBCL includes multiple entities including: mucosa-associated lymphoid tissue (MALT) lymphoma, splenic lymphoma with or without villous lymphocytes (SLV2), and nodal marginal zone lymphoma. This is considered an indolent lymphoma, and in fact, splenectomy is sometimes curative. A conservative approach is taken in many patients, with either not receiving chemotherapy, splenectomy alone, or sometimes with chemotherapy at the time of diagnosis. Nevertheless, most patients will have a long, minimally progressive course to their disease. Some reports indicate that as many as 60% will not have significant progression is spite of the conservative approaches taken, with median event-free survivals of 6.9 years. The overall median survival is approximately 9 years.

Clinical Features

History:

Splenic MZBCL is usually an indolent disease and has an insidious onset. It is common for this disorder to be discovered incidentally during a routine physical examination on a hematology profile. Most cases of are associated with peripheral blood involvement. Other salient features include:

- Most common in adults
- Median age in the 60s
- Female predominance
- A feeling of fullness

Physical:

- Usually massive splenomegaly
- Minimal, or absent lymphadenopathy
- Bone marrow commonly involved, but not extensive
- Most present with stage IV disease

Complications:

- Splenomegaly and lymphocytosis are common, and may present a clinical picture mimicking other lymphomas.
- Hyper IgM (an M spike) is present in 25% of cases.
- Cytopenias in MZBCL worsen with further enlargement, probably secondary to splenic destruction and cell lysis. A positive Coomb's test is present in 15% of cases, thus autoimmune hemolytic anemia is included in the differential diagnosis of anemia in MZBCL.
- Thrombocytopenia is usually caused by bone marrow involvement, splenic sequestration, and immune thrombocytopenia.

Laboratory Workup

- Complete blood count with differential shows circulating lymphoma cells in 60% of cases, but an absolute lymphocytosis of >5000 lymphocytes/μl is not always present.
- Microscopic examination of peripheral blood smear may show villous lymphocytes, or non-villous lymphocytes with considerable morphologic heterogeneity.
- Bone marrow aspiration/biopsy is not required in all cases, but may be necessary in selected cases to establish the diagnosis as well as to assess other complicating features such as the differential diagnosis of thrombocytopenia (destruction versus hypoproduction).
- Splenectomy is required for painful spleen, and for diagnostic histopathology, and may be curative.

Morphology

The peripheral blood lymphoma cells typically range from small to medium in size with round to oval nuclei, prominent nucleoli and moderate amounts of pale cytoplasm. These features may cause confusion with hairy cell leukemia. In general, these cells are a little larger than normal lymphocytes.

Bone marrow involvement may the form of small paratrabecular lymphoid aggregates (Figure 4.4), but may also be contain small nodules throughout. The marrow involvement is usually disproportionately low for the number of circulating cells, as these come mainly from the spleen. Marrow aspirates nicely demonstrate the morphologic features.

Histologic sections of the spleen demonstrate white pulp nodules with a central core of small lymphoid cells surrounded by a pale rim of splenic marginal zone cells, with or without residual follicular centers. A normal mantle zone is absent.

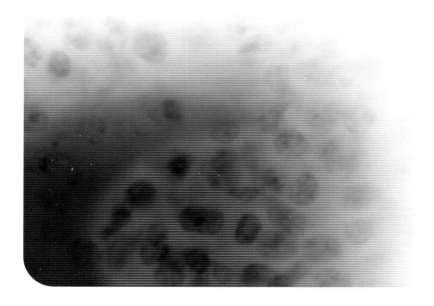

Immunophenotype / Differential Diagnosis

The major immunophenotypic differential includes HCL, B-PLL and B-CLL/SLL with variable morphology. The diagnosis is most reliably made by the combined clinical, morphologic and immunophenotypic features. The presence of distinct nucleoli, absence of reticulin fibrosis in the marrow and predominant splenic white pulp involvement point to MZBCL as opposed to HCL. The CD11c+/25+/103+ profile of HCL is not seen, although individual antigens in the HCL group may be present. The smooth cytoplasmic borders and distinct macronucleoli of B-PLL are useful to distinguish it from MZBCL. While both are FMC7+ and a significant minority CD5+, the presence of CD103 and/or CD11c should point towards HCL. Lastly, in a majority of cases of MZBCL, either CD5 and/or CD23 are absent, in distinction to B-CLL/SLL.

- The most common immunophenotype of splenic MZBCL includes positivity for the B-cell antigens CD19, CD20, CD22, FMC7, and strong sIg.
- Most cases are CD5-, CD10-, CD11c-, CD103-, and usually CD23-.
- Hairy cell leukemia can be usually be eliminated by the lack of CD11c, CD103, and usually CD25.

Genetics

Cells in splenic MZBCL have both Ig heavy and light chain genes clonally rearranged. There are no specific genetic abnormalities in this disease.

Pearls of Immunophenotyping Splenic MZBCL

Pearl 1: The malignant lymphocytes are B-cells expressing CD19 and CD20 equally.

Pearl 2: There is not specific pattern that is diagnostic.

Pearl 3: Combined histology/morphology and immunophenotype are needed for diagnosis.

References

Swerdlow SH: Small B-cell lymphomas of the lymph nodes and spleen: Practical insights to diagnosis and pathogenesis. Mod Pathol 12:125-140, 1998.

Jaffe ES, Harris NL, Diebold J et al. World Health Organization Classification of Neoplastic Diseases of the Hematopoietic and Lymphoid tissues A Progress Report. Am J Clin Pathol 1999; 111 (Suppl.1):pp. S8-S12

Harris NL, Jaffe ES, Stein H et al: A revised European-American classification of lymphoid neoplasms: A proposal from the international lymphoma study group. Blood 84: 1361-1392, 1994.

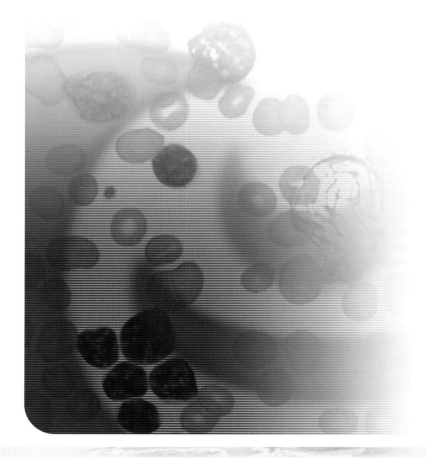

Man With Enlarging Belt Size

Case Presentation

casefive

A 57 year old man came to his primary care physician claiming to be feeling just fine, except that for the past few months his belt size had been increasing even though he was not gaining weight. In fact, he had lost about 5 pounds since his last exam 6 months ago. He said this was because he felt really full after only a small meal. Also, he had noted that it took up to half an hour sometimes to quit bleeding if he cut himself shaving. On physical examination, he did in fact appear to be in good physical shape for his age, but had a markedly enlarged spleen and a mildly enlarged liver.

As part of his examination, his physician ordered a hematology profile to check his platelet count.

TABLE 5.1 – MAXM® Results

- WBC: 3.1 K/µL
- Platelets: 40 K/µL
- RBC: 3.70 M/µL
- RDW: 15.9 units
- Hemoglobin: 9.9 g/dL
- Hematocrit: 29.8 %

Suspect flags: Monocytosis.

Definitive flags: Thrombocytopenia, Leukopenia.

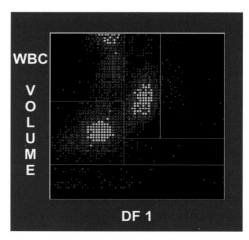

Figure 5.1 Automated WBC differential from a MAXM.

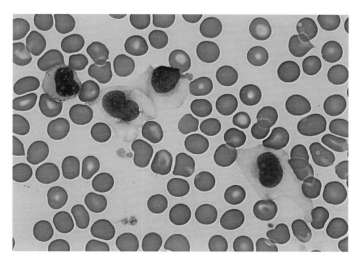

Figure 5.2 Peripheral Blood, Wright-Giemsa stain.

The WBC histogram from the MAXM® revealed an interesting pattern of cells in the DF 1 display that showed a population of cells high in volume in the monocyte region (Figure 5.1). A manual slide review (Figure 5.2) showed some small, compact lymphocytes present, but also larger mononuclear cells with more abundant pale cytoplasm, and mainly oval or kidney-shaped nuclei with small nucleoli. These were thought to be larger lymphoid cells rather than monocytes.

A flow cytometric examination of peripheral blood was ordered to further evaluate this cell population. Pertinent histograms and data from 3-color immunophenotyping are shown (Figure 5.3).

CD20 and CD19 are similar in their positivity, with a CD19:CD20 percent-positive ratio of 1, but the CD20 intensity of antigen expression is very prominent. FMC7, as well as CD11c and CD103, is expressed on most of the CD19+ cells. CD5 and CD23 are absent. Bright expression of immunoglobulin light chain kappa is present. The reported immunophenotype of this lymphocytosis is: CD5-, CD19+, CD20+, CD23-, FMC7+, CD11c+, and CD103+, with monoclonal kappa light chain expression.

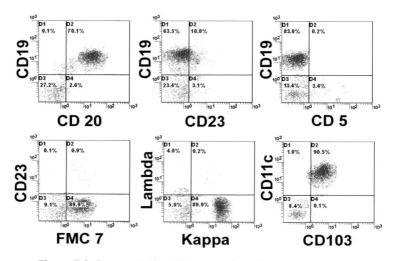

Figure 5.3 Representative historgrams from flow cytometry.

On the basis of these findings, and the pancytopenia, a bone marrow aspiration and biopsy were attempted, although the physician was unable to acquire aspirated marrow. Figure 5.4 shows the characteristic histology.

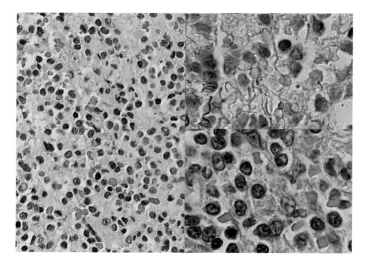

Figure 5.4 Bone Marrow Biopsy. The left panel shows a lower power view with H+E stain. The right panel shows a higher power view (lower right) and a reticulin stain (upper right).

On the basis of these findings, and probable clinical improvement, a splenectomy was performed. The splenic histology was similar to that of the bone marrow such that no repeat flow cytometric studies were necessary from the spleen.

Hairy Cell Leukemia

Introduction

Hairy cell leukemia (HCL) is one of the lymphomas involving significant splenomegaly. Others include: B-cell prolymphocytic leukemia (B-PLL), splenic marginal zone lymphoma, and variant HCL (vHCL). HCL was described in the Revised European American Lymphoma (REAL) classification, and is included in the World Health Organization (WHO) classification system. This disease is uncommon, but when seen, it usually affects middle-aged men, who almost always present with splenomegaly and pancytopenia. Hepatomegaly is fairly common, but lymphadenopathy is uncommon. Most deaths are due to infections typically associated with neutropenia. The median survival is 5 years, with neutropenia predicting the group at highest risk for death. Those without neutropenia often survive for over ten years. Treatments with interferon-alpha, nucleoside analogs and/or pentostatin can induce durable remissions in most patients, and some are cured because it is curable.

Clinical Features

History:

HCL is uncommon, but is important to recognize. Most cases of are associated with pancytopenia and peripheral blood involvement. Other salient features include:

- Most common in middle-aged males
- A feeling of fullness from organomegaly
- Common presenting signs are manifestations of cytopenias, including bleeding, fatigue, and fever.

Physical:

- Usually massive splenomegaly
- Hepatomegaly usually minimal
- Minimal, or absent lymphadenopathy
- Bone marrow is commonly involved

Complications:

- Infections and fever from neutropenia
- Bleeding and hemorrhage from thrombocytopenia
- Fatigue and/or cardiopulmonary difficulties from anemia

Laboratory Workup

- Complete blood count commonly shows one or more cytopenias, but an absolute lymphocytosis of >5000 lymphocytes/µl is uncommon.
- Microscopic examination of peripheral blood smear may show only occasional neoplastic cells.
- A tartrate-resistant acid phosphatase (TRAP) stain is useful in diagnosis.
- Bone marrow aspiration/biopsy should be performed in virtually all cases of pancytopenia, and may also be necessary to establish the diagnosis and assess other complicating features such as the extent of marrow replacement.
- Splenectomy is required for painful spleen, and for diagnostic histopathology, and may help resolve the cytopenias.

Morphology

The peripheral blood HCL cells are typically of medium or large size with oval or reniform nuclei containing a dispersed, spongy, chromatin pattern, indistinct nucleoli and moderate to prominent amounts of pale cytoplasm. In some cases, the cytoplasmic projections (hairy cells) are readily visible, while in others (such as this case) they are indistinct. These features may cause confusion with other spleen-based lymphomas such as MZBCL. In general, these cells are larger than normal lymphocytes, and typically fall in the monocyte region in automated hematology analyzers.

As noted, the TRAP stain can be quite useful in assessment of suspected HCL in the blood. Before immunophenotyping came into use, the diagnosis of HCL was confirmed by strong diffuse TRAP reactivity in the neoplastic cells (Figure 5.5). It should be pointed out that weak to moderate TRAP reactivity may also be observed in benign lymphocytes of Epstein-Barr Virus infections, and in lymphoid cells of Sezary syndrome, B-PLL and B-CLL/SLL.

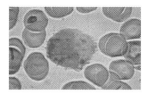

Figure 5.5 Peripheral Blood, positive tartrate-resistant acid phosphatase (TRAP) stain.

Aspiration of bone marrow is frequently difficult as a result of reticulin fibrosis. Thus, marrow biopsies are invaluable for diagnosis. Involvement is sometimes nodular, but more commonly involves a diffuse, patchy pattern or diffuse infiltration throughout. Sometimes, in the case of minimal involvement, the patches are difficult to identify. Some describe the biopsy pattern of histology as a "fried egg" appearance due to the abundant, poorly-stained cytoplasm. The spleen is typically replaced by HCL.

Immunophenotype / Differential Diagnosis

The immunophenotypic differential diagnosis of HCL includes the spleen-based lymphomas, B-PLL and MZBCL, but also B-CLL/SLL with variable morphology. The diagnosis should rely on combined clinical, morphologic and immunophenotypic features. With the exception of HCL, these other splenic lymphomas do not have characteristic immunophenotypes, cytogenetic or genotypic features.

HCL cells usually have a bright CD45 expression, as do other mature B lymphoid leukemias. The forward, and particularly the side light scatter are increased to the extent light scatter plots resemble large lymphoid cells or monocytes, not unlike the situation with the volume parameter on hematology instruments.

HCL is one of the few lymphoid leukemias whose immunophenotypic profile may be considered "diagnostic" by itself. First, HCL strongly expresses the major B cell antigens (CD19, 20, 22), including sIg.

A relatively unique feature of the hairy cells is the bright expression of CD11c, CD22, CD103 and FMC7. The bright expression of CD11c and CD103 is very specific for HCL in the setting of a monoclonal B lymphoproliferation. Most HCLs fail to express CD5 or CD10.

CD25 is present in approximately 70-80% of cases, and is typically dim to moderate in intensity.

Genetics

Cells in HCL have both Ig heavy and light chain genes clonally rearranged, but there are no specific genetic abnormalities in this disease. In a significant fraction of cases, sIg will be present as multiple, atypical combinations of heavy chain isotypes IgG, IgA, IgM, and IgD (e.g. IgA/IgG/IgD positive). Functional studies have suggested that HCL represents cells "frozen" at a post-proliferative, but pre-plasmacytic stage of B cell maturation, a stage in which immunoglobulin isotype switching occurs.

Pearls of Immunophenotyping HCL

Pearl 1: The malignant lymphocytes are B-cells expressing CD19 and CD20 equally., with bright sIg.

Pearl 2: A characteristic feature of HCL is the bright expression of CD11c, CD22, CD103 and FMC7.

Pearl 3: The TRAP stain is useful in diagnosis of HCL.

References

Swerdlow SH: Small B-cell lymphomas of the lymph nodes and spleen: Practical insights to diagnosis and pathogenesis. Mod Pathol 12:125-140, 1998.

Jaffe ES, Harris NL, Diebold J et al. World Health Organization Classification of Neoplastic Diseases of the Hematopoietic and Lymphoid tissues A Progress Report. Am J Clin Pathol 1999; 111 (Suppl.1):pp. S8-S12

Harris NL, Jaffe ES, Stein H et al: A revised European-American classification of lymphoid neoplasms: A proposal from the international lymphoma study group. Blood 84: 1361-1392, 1994.

Man With Rouleax on Smear

Case Presentation

A 77 year old man came to his primary care physician for his regularly scheduled examination. He had been mildly anemic six months prior, and had been placed on iron and multivitamin supplementation. His hematology profile was reported from the laboratory showing prominent Rouleax formation of RBCs and a prominent lymphocytosis. Review of the peripheral smear by the pathologist suggested the possibility of a low-grade lymphoma, favoring early stage B-CLL/SLL.

The WBC histogram from the MAXM® revealed an interesting pattern of cells in the DF 1 display that showed a prominent population of cells in the lymphoid region, but with lack of sharp delineation between cell peaks (Figure 6.1), consistent with the blood smear morphology (Figure 6.2).

TABLE 6.1 – MAXM® Results

- WBC: 38.1 K/µL
- Platelets: 140 K/µL
- RBC: 3.60 M/µL
- RDW: 15.9 units
- Hemoglobin: 9.7 g/dL
- Hematocrit: 29.8 %

Suspect flags: Variant lymphs.

Definitive flags: Thrombocytopenia, Leukocytosis.

casesix

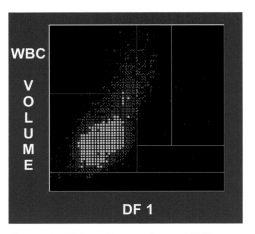

Figure 6.1 WBC scattergram from a MAXM.

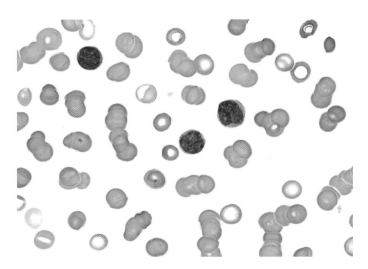

Figure 6.2 Peripheral Blood, Wright-Giemsa stain.

A flow cytometric examination of peripheral blood was ordered to further evaluate this lymphoid cell population. Pertinent histograms and data from 3-color immunophenotyping are shown (Figure 6.3).

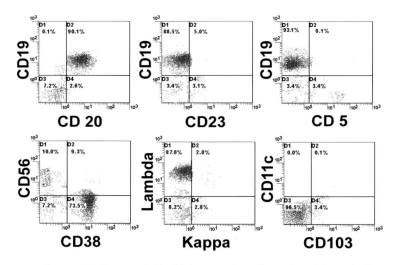

Figure 6.3 Representative histograms from flow cytometric analysis.

CD20 and CD19 are similar in their positivity, with a CD19:CD20 per-cent-positive ratio of ~1. CD38 is expressed on most cells, while CD5 and CD23 are absent. Bright immunoglobulin light chain expression of lambda is present. The reported immunophenotype of this lymphocytosis is: CD19+, CD20+, CD38+, CD5-, CD23-, CD11c-, and CD103-, with mono-clonal kappa light chain expression.

On the basis of these findings, a bone marrow aspiration and biopsy were performed to determine the extent of disease.

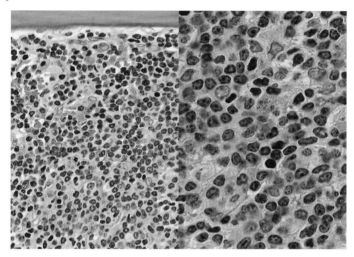

Figure 6.4 Bone Marrow Biopsy. The left panel shows a lower power view with H+E stain. The right panel shows a higher power view.

Lymphoplasmacytic Lymphoma

Introduction

Lymphoplasmacytic Lymphoma (LPL) is a rare small B-cell lymphoma with plasmacytic differentiation that is sometimes difficult to categorize. The bone marrow, lymph nodes, and spleen are frequently involved. Peripheral blood is involved less frequently. As currently defined, it is important to rule out B-CLL/SLL with plasmacytoid features, as well as FL or MZBCL with plasmacytoid features. Most patients with LPL have a monoclonal IgM paraprotein and the syndrome of Waldenstrom's macroglobulinemia, consistent with the prominent Rouleax formation in the blood. The disease is usually clinically indolent, but transformation to a large cell lymphoma may also occur.

Clinical Features

History:

LPL is an uncommon and usually indolent disease, but is important to recognize, in that it is more aggressive than B-CLL/SLL. Cells of LPL often secrete IgM, and the condition is called Waldenstrom's macroglobulinemia (WM). Bone involvement is almost always seen.

Physical:

- The spleen, lymph nodes, and bone marrow are frequently involved, less commonly found in blood.

Complications:

- The presence of significant quantities of IgM, a large protein, in the blood may produce hyperviscosity symptoms such as bleeding, confusion, fatigue, and oncotic plasma volume expansion.

Laboratory Workup

- Complete blood count commonly shows one or more cytopenias, with wide variation in the absolute lymphocyte count.
- Microscopic examination of peripheral blood smear typically shows prominent Rouleax formation of RBCs in cases with Waldenstrom's macroglobulinemia.
- Quantitative serum immunoglobulin levels and immunofixation are helpful in diagnosis and monitoring of LPL treatment.
- Bone marrow aspiration/biopsy should be performed in virtually all cases of pancytopenia, and may also be necessary to establish the diagnosis and to assess other complicating features such as the extent of marrow replacement.
- Splenectomy is required for painful spleen, and for diagnostic histopathology.

Morphology

Morphologically, LPL is comprised of small lymphocytes, plasmacytoid lymphocytes, and plasma cells, and by definition lacks features diagnostic of B-CLL/SLL, MCL, FL, and MZBCL. Plasmacytoid lymphocytes and plasma cells may be admixed with small lymphocytes. In some cases, intranuclear inclusions of PAS-positive Ig (Dutcher bodies) may be seen. In the bone marrow, LPL may be observed as poorly defined aggregates or, as in this case, diffuse replacement of the marrow by small lymphocytes, plasmacytoid lymphocytes and occasional plasma cells.

Immunophenotype / Differential Diagnosis

The differential diagnosis includes typical IgM monoclonal gammopathy of unknown significance (MGUS), B-CLL/SLL, and anaplastic multiple myeloma. CD19, CD20 and sIg are positive in LPL with WM and negative in multiple myeloma. The isotype of the proteinemia also differs: IgM in Waldenstrom's, and IgG or IgA in myeloma. Those cases of LPL with a CLL-like morphology are usually CD5- and CD23-, although some cases will express either one or the other. B-CLL/SLL cases are almost always CD5+ and CD23+, and usually have very small IgM monoclonal gammopathies of much less than 1 gm/dL. IgM MGUS cases are usually differentiated from LPL with WM on the basis of the serum IgM concentration.

- The LPL cells have an immunophenotype demonstrating plasma cell-associated antigens such as CD38, as well as CD19, CD20, CD22, CD45 (dim to brightly), sIg, and sometimes FMC7.
- LPL is usually negative for CD5 and CD23, which rules out B-CLL/SLL..

Genetics

LPL usually demonstrates clonal rearrangement of both Ig heavy and light chain genes with somatic mutation, suggesting a post-antigen-stimulated stage of differentiation. Approximately 50% of LPL demonstrate a t(9;14)(p13;q32) translocation that involves a B-cell-specific transcription factor, (PAX-5) gene and the Ig heavy chain locus.

Pearls of Immunophenotyping LPL

Pearl 1: The malignant lymphocytes are B-cells expressing CD19 and CD20, but also have features of plasmacytic differentiation such as CD38 expression and cIg in some cells.

Pearl 2: LPL can be distinguished from B-CLL/SLL using CD5 and CD23.

References

Swerdlow SH: Small B-cell lymphomas of the lymph nodes and spleen: Practical insights to diagnosis and pathogenesis. Mod Pathol 12:125-140, 1998.

Jaffe ES, Harris NL, Diebold J et al. World Health Organization Classification of Neoplastic Diseases of the Hematopoietic and Lymphoid tissues A Progress Report. Am J Clin Pathol 1999; 111 (Suppl.1):pp. S8-S12

Harris NL, Jaffe ES, Stein H et al: A revised European-American classification of lymphoid neoplasms: A proposal from the international lymphoma study group. Blood 84: 1361-1392, 1994.

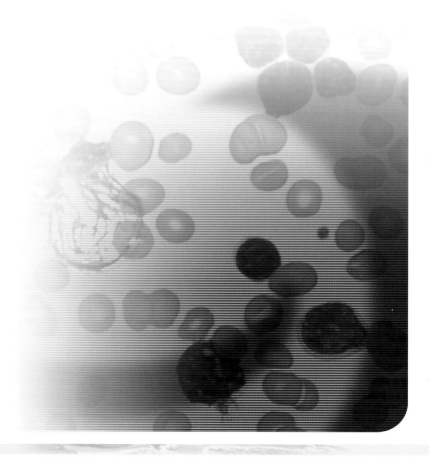

Boy With Pancytopenia

Case Presentation

Five days before admission to the hospital, this previously healthy 13-year-old boy developed a fever, sore throat, chills, and generalized muscle pain (myalgias). Three days prior to admission, he was noted to have a reddened sore throat, and was administered amoxicillin. The throat culture was negative for beta-streptococcus. Because his fever persisted, he was examined at the local hospital further and found to have a fine erythematous rash that started on both his arms and legs simultaneously. The hematology examination included: WBC 3,200/µL, hemoglobin 11.7 g/dL, platelet count 49,000/µL, and a differential with 91% polymorphonuclear neutrophils (PMNs), 2% bands, and 7% lymphocytes. He related a history of tick bites approximately 2 weeks prior, and thus was thought to have Rocky Mountain spotted fever.

He was admitted to the hospital, all antibiotics were discontinued for 24 hours, and blood cultures were obtained. After the initial 24 hours, he was started on intravenous doxycycline (100 mg every 12 hours) for 4 days, followed by 5 days of oral doxycycline. His fever rapidly normalized over the first 48 hours, and he remained afebrile. As part of his evaluation, daily hematology profiles were used to determine normalization of

TABLE 7.1 – MAXM® Results

- WBC: 18.6 K/µL
- PMNs: 8%
- Lymphocytes: 88%
- Platelets: 205 K/µL
- Hemoglobin: 10.7 g/dL
- Hematocrit: 31%

Suspect flags: Blasts, Variant lymphs.

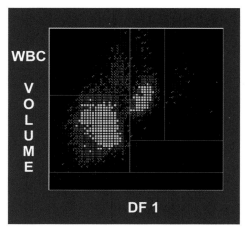

Figure 7.1 Scattergram from MAXM.

caseseven

his cytopenias. During the first 5 days of hospitalization, his WBC changed from 3,200 with 91% PMNs and 7% lymphocytes, to data from the 6th day of hospitalization, as shown.

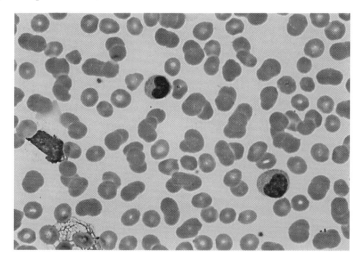

Figure 7.2 Peripheral Blood, Wright-Giemsa stain.

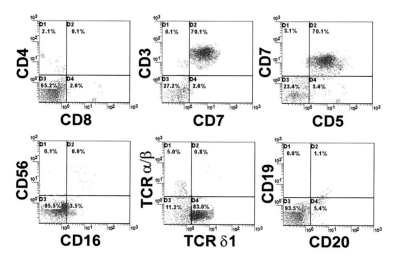

Figure 7.3 A flow cytometric examination of peripheral blood was ordered to further evaluate this lymphocytosis. Pertinent histograms and data from 3-color immunophenotyping are shown.

The WBC histogram from the MAXM revealed an unusual pattern of cells that suggested a heterogeneous pattern in the DF 1 display in the lymphoid region (Figure 7.1). Upon a manual slide review (Figure 7.2), there were certainly small, compact lymphocytes present, but also intermediate and larger lymphoid cells with cleaved or reniform nuclei and mature chromatin clumping present, and many cells contained azurophilic cytoplasmic granules. With the possibility of lymphoma, flow cytometric analysis was ordered.

Of notice, while CD8 and CD4 are only minimally present, these cells are positive for CD3, CD5, and CD7 (Figure 7.3). The intensity of CD3 is bright, while that of CD5 is dimmer than on typical mature T-cells. Histograms of CD16 and CD56 show virtually no staining, similar to the CD19/CD20 combination. However, the histogram of TCRδ1 and TCR α/β shows these cells to be expressing the δTCR chain, but not the α/β heterodimer. Thus, the reported immunophenotype of this lymphocytosis is: CD3+, CD5+, CD7+, CD4-, CD8-, and positive for TCRδ1.

Additional immunostaining with a panel of monoclonal antibodies directed against several variable region gene products of the TCR was also performed. In the case of the γ chain, the cells were positive for Vγ9 (clone IMMU 360), and for Vδ2 (clone IMMU 389. Thus, these cells were clonally expanded, as is sometimes seen in mycobacterial infections.

Ehrlichia chaffeensis Infection

Introduction

Human ehrlichiosis, caused by E. chaffeensis, is a tick-borne infectious disease commonly referred to as human monocytic ehrlichiosis (HME). HME may produce a serious febrile illness which is sometimes fatal. Most cases, however, resolve spontaneously via an immune response not yet fully characterized. Such individuals suffer flu-like symptoms, and only a small percentage of infected people actually seek medical attention for severe or protracted illness. Of those seriously infected patients, most are readily treated and cured by doxycycline, but persistent infection and death have been recorded. A profound lymphocytosis occurs in many of those with acute ehrlichiosis during successful treatment with doxycycline.

Little is known about naturally-occurring immune responses in HME. In part, this is a reflection of the self-limited nature of most infections and no good animal model of human infection with E. chaffeensis exists to study these issues. Studies of a number of patients immediately before, and following, appropriate antibiotic treatment with doxycycline show an unusual and sometimes profound lymphocytosis of γ/δ T-cells, characterized as CD3+4-8- Vγ9/Vδ2, which accompanies the period of recovery from acute infection.

Ehrlichiosis, as well as several other intracellular infections, is accompanied by a rapid increase in γ/δ T-cells. This response begins within a few hours of initiation of treatment and steadily increases in some patients with HME to a peak at 5-12 days following therapy, but complete resolution and return to a normal lymphocyte subset distribution may take as long as 4 weeks. Prior to treatment, most patients are lymphopenic, with markedly low CD4 and CD8 subsets.

The role of doxycycline in this recovery process has not been examined in detail. Since all the patients studied were treated, it has not been possible to determine what (if any) role this antibiotic plays in the recovery phase of acute ehrlichiosis. However, when patients were examined prior to initiation of treatment, they were typically lymphopenic and their lymphocyte subsets produced virtually no measurable IFN-γ and/or IL-4. Within the first 24 hours, however, intracellular IL-4 production became apparent. Thus, it is possible that doxycycline had some direct effect on the immune response, but may also have merely released some ehrlichia-related immune suppression.

Most intracellular infections involve a usually minor subpopulation of T cells expressing the γ/δ TCR. These CD3+ cells generally do not express CD4 or CD8, nor require major histocompatibility complex (MHC) antigens for function. They show a broad cytotoxicity against autologous cells infected with intracellular pathogens. Although studied intensely in recent times, the role(s) of γ/δ T cells is not entirely clear. Recent reports suggest that γ/δ T cells can play a "front line" defensive role early in infections and direct secretion of specific cytokines that produce either a Th1 or Th2 immune response.

Clinical Features

History:

Infections with E. chaffeensis produce a wide range of symptoms and signs at presentation. In general, this infection occurs predominantly in the eastern half of the US, and mainly in the middle to southern states. The organism is carried by certain types of ticks that utilize the white-tailed deer as a reservoir. Thus, a history of tick bites preceeding the clinical disease is common. Other salient features include:

- Reported most commonly in adults, but also occasionally in children
- Usually presents with a flu-like illness
- May present with acute onset of fever, chills and headache
- Most cases resolve spontaneously without hospitalization

Physical:

- May have mild localized or generalized lymphadenopathy
- Often accompanied by nausea, myalgias, arthralgias, and malaise
- A subset of patients experience prolonged fever ranging from 17-57 days
- Some patients have central nervous system (CNS) manifestations

Complications:

- Extensive, febrile illness can result in hositalization and death.
- Most complications are those of cytopenias.
- CNS manifestations include confusion, delerium, headache, or overt meningitis.

Laboratory Workup

- Complete blood count with differential shows absolute lymphopenia in early phase of infection, along with neutropenia, thrombocytopenia and anemia, or some combination of these.
- Elevations of hepatic enzymes are common.
- Visualization of organisms in blood smears is uncommon.
- Definitive diagnosis is by PCR for E. chaffeensis
- Bone marrow aspiration/biopsy is not required, other than in selected atypical cases to assess other complicating features such as the differential diagnosis of thrombocytopenia (destruction versus hypoproduction).
- Lymph node or soft tissue biopsy is not required.

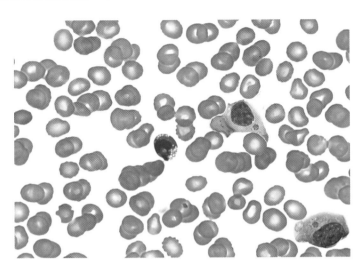

Figure 7.4 Peripheral Blood, Wright-Giemsa stain. Mononuclear cells contatin morulae of E. chaffeensis.

Morphology

The peripheral blood lymphocytes in HME are typically comprised of small-to-medium size with oval to reniform-shaped nuclei, small nucleoli and moderate amounts of cytoplasm containing azurophilic granules. They can be quite variable in size, ranging from small lymphocytes to also include larger cells with more abundant cytoplasm and nuclear heterogeneity including prominent nucleoli.

Visualization of the morulae of E. chaffeensis is helpful, when present, but this is an uncommon event (Figure 7.4).

If a bone marrow is performed, involvement is typical and organisms can best be detected by immunohistochemical staining for E. chaffeensis.

Immunophenotype / Differential Diagnosis

The diagnosis of HME may be strongly suspected from the clinical presentation and initial laboratory data. In children, any other low-grade lymphoma would be unlikely. However, in older adults, the differential diagnosis should include circulating lymphomas. Additional immunophenotyping and/or genotyping could be used to rule out malignancy. Definitive testing for E. chaffeensis by PCR is very helpful.

- The most common immunophenotype in HME is CD3+, CD5+, CD7+, CD4-, CD8-, and positive for the γ/δ T-cell receptor.
- The immunophenotypic differential diagnosis of HME in adults includes all small lymphoid neoplasms of T-cell type, but mainly T-cell CLL/SLL and Large Granular Lymphocytic Leukemia.

Genetics

These cells are oligoclonal T cells expressing the γ/δ T-cell receptor, expressing restriction to Vγ9 and Vδ2.

Pearls of Immunophenotyping E. chaffeensis:

Pearl 1: During the initial acute lymphopenic phase, the T-cells are mainly CD3+/CD4+, or CD3+/CD8+.

Pearl 2: A lymphocytosis ensues 1-4 days following initiation of doxycycline.

Pearl 3: The T-cells during the lymphocytosis are characterized as CD3+4-8-Vγ9+/Vδ2+.

Pearl 4: Within 1-3 days of the peak lymphocyte count, normal CD3+/CD4+, and CD3+/CD8+ start to return.

Pearl 5: Normalization of immunophenotype may take as long as 4 weeks.

References

Caldwell CW, Poje E, Cooperstock M: Expansion of immature thymic precursor cells in peripheral blood following acute marrow suppression. Am J Clin Pathol 95:824-827, 1991.

Roland WE, McDonald G, Caldwell CW, et al: Ehrlichiosis - a cause of prolonged fever. Clin Infect Dis 20:281, 1995.

Caldwell CW, Everett ED, McDonald G, et al: Lymphocytosis of γ/δ T Cells in human ehrlichiosis. Am J Clin Pathol 103:761, 1995.

Caldwell CW, Everett ED, McDonald G, et al: Apoptosis of γ/δ T Cells in human ehrlichiosis. Am J Clin Pathol 105:640, 1996.

Rathnasamy N, Everett ED, Roland WE, et al: Central nervous system manifestations of human ehrlichiosis. Clin Infect Disease 23:314-319, 1996.

Useful Lymphoid CD Reagents

Predominantly T-Cells

Cluster Designation	Function	Cell Distribution	Disease Association
CD2	• Intracellular adhesion, ligand for CD58	• All normal mature T-cells • Most NK cells	• Mature T-cell and NK-Cell neoplasms
CD3	• Antigen binding and signal transduction complex	• All functional T-cells	• Mature T-cell neoplasms
CD4	• Major Histocompatibility Class II-restricted antigen recognition • HIV receptor	• Helper/Inducer T-cells • Weakly expressed on monocytes	• Some mature T-cell lymphomas, Most T-cell CLL/SLL, T-PLL, Adult T-cell leukemia/lymphoma • Sezary syndrome Mycosis fungoides
CD5	• T-cell proliferation • Ligand for CD72	• Minor B-cell subset • Most thymocytes • All normal, mature T-cells	• B-cell CLL/SLL • Mantle cell lymphoma • Most T-cell neoplasms
CD7	• T and NK cell activation	• Early T-cell antigen that persists on most mature T-cells	• Most T-cell neoplasms • May be absent in Sezary syndrome/Mycosis fungoides
CD8	• Major Histocompatibility Complex class I- restricted antigen recognition	• T-suppressor/cytotoxic cells • Some NK cells	• Some mature T-cell neoplasms • Large granular lymphocytic leukemia
TCR α/β	• T-cell receptor α/β heterodimer	• Most mature, circulating T-cells (95-99%)	• Most T-cell neoplasms that express CD3
TCR γ/δ	• T-cell receptor γ/δ heterodimer	• Some thymocytes • A few mature circulating T-cells (1-5%)	• Rare mature T-cell neoplasms • Some lymphoblastic lymphomas

Useful Lymphoid CD Reagents

Predominantly B-Cells

Cluster Designation	Function	Cell Distribution	Disease Association
CD10	• Hydrolyzes biologically active peptides	• Early B and T-cells • Follicular center cells	• Precursor B-cell ALL • Follicular lymphoma
CD19	• B-cell activation/proliferation • Associates with CD21 for signal transduction in B-cells	• All B-cells • Expressed at the time of immunoglobulin heavy chain gene arrangement and present until terminal differentiation into a plasma cell	• B-cell ALL • Mature B-cell neoplasms • Usually absent in plasma cell neoplasms
CD20	• B-cell activation/proliferation	• Mature B-cells • Expressed at the time of immunoglobulin light chain gene arrangement	• Some B-cell ALL • Most mature B-cell neoplasms • Usually absent in plasma cell neoplasms
CD22	• B-cell activation/proliferation	• Mature B-cells	• Some B-cell ALL • Most mature B-cell neoplasms
CD23	• Low affinity IgE receptor	• Mature B-cells	• B-cell CLL/SLL • Usually absent in mantle cell lymphoma

Useful Lymphoid CD Reagents

Miscellaneous CDs

Cluster Designation	Function	Cell Distribution	Disease Association
CD11c	• Cell-cell and cell-matrix adhesion • Fibrinogen binding "CR4"	• Monocytes • Granulocytes	• Hairy cell leukemia • Splenic marginal zone lymphoma • Some other B-cell neoplasms
CD16	• Low affinity receptor for aggregated IgG • NK signal transduction, macrophage phagocytosis	• NK-cells • Neutrophils • Monocytes	• Large granular lymphocytic leukemia
CD25	• Low affinity IL-2 receptor • Induces activation and proliferation of T-cells	• Activated T-cells, B-cells, NK-cells • Monocytes	• Adult T-cell leukemia/lymphoma • Hairy cell leukemia
CD38	• Leukocyte activation	• Early T- and B-cells • Activated T- and B-cells • Plasma cells	• Plasmacytic neoplasms • Some B-cell lymphomas
CD56	• Mediates NK:target cell adhesion	• NK-cells	• Large granular lymphocytic leukemia
CD57		• NK-cells • Some T and B-cells	• Large granular lymphocytic leukemia
CD103		• Activated T-cells	• Hairy cell leukemia • Some splenic lymphomas
FMC-7		• Some B-cells	• Prolymphocytic leukemia • Hairy cell leukemia • Splenic lymphomas

These CDs are intended only as a general guide to those that have utility in evaluation of lymphocytosis. Others, and in various combinations of multi-color fluorochromes should be decided on an individual laboratory basis.

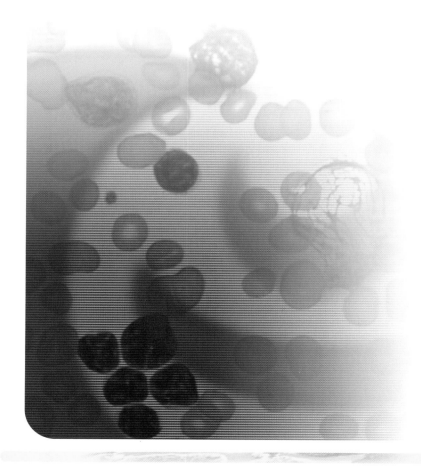

B-Cell Malignancies

Diagnosis	Immunophenotype	Genotype	Clinical Features
B-Cell Chronic Lymphocytic Leukemia/Small Lymphocytic Lymphoma	CD19+, CD20+, CD5+, CD23 +, Dim IgM+, CD38+/- CD20% < CD19%	Trisomy 12, Deletions at 11q23, Abnormalities of 13q	Older patients, usually with widespread disease and blood involvement. CD38 helps distinguish between slowly and rapidly progressive disease.
Follicular Lymphoma	CD19+, CD20+, CD10+, CD5-, Bright Ig, mainly IgG	t(14;18) involving BCL2 gene	Older patients with generalized adenopathy and marrow involvement.
Mantle Cell Lymphoma	CD19+, CD20+, CD5+, CD23- CD10-, sIgM+/IgD+	t(11;14) involves overexpression of BCL1 (cyclin D1)	Older patients with generalized adenopathy and marrow involvement. May arise at extranodal sites and spleen.
Marginal Zone Lymphoma	CD19+, CD20+, CD5- CD10-, CD23-, sIg+, cIg+/-	Trisomy 18, t(11;18)	Frequently arises in extranodal sites in adult patients with chronic inflammatory diseases. Tends to remain localized for long time.
Hairy Cell Leukemia	CD19+, CD20+, CD11c+, CD25+, CD103+, and Bright sIg+, Bright CD20	None specific	Older males with pancytopenia typically.
B-Cell Prolymphocytic Leukemia	CD19+, CD20+, Bright sIg, Bright HLA-Dr	None specific	Rare disease with prominent splenomegaly.
Lymphoplasmacytic Lymphoma	CD19+, CD20+, sIg (usually IgM) CD5-, CD10-, CD23-	t(9;14) in 50 percent (PAX 5 gene)	Older patients. Hyperviscosity.

T-Cell Malignancies

Diagnosis	Immunophenotype	Genotype	Clinical Feature
T- Cell Chronic Lymphocytic Leukemia/Small Lymphocytic Lymphoma	Pan-T markers positive,may be CD4+ or CD8+. CD1-, TdT-	Clonal TCR rearrangements	T-CLL/SLL is rare. Usually adults with generalized lymphadenopathy and bone marrow involvement.
Adult T-Cell Leukemia/Lymphoma	Pan-T markers positive, usually CD4+, CD25+	HTLV-1 provirus present	Adults with cutaneous lesions, marrow involvement, and hypercalcemia.
Mycosis Fungoides/Sezary Syndrome	CD3+, CD4+, a/b TCR+, usually CD7-	None Specific	Adults with cutaneous patches, plaques, nodules or generalized erythrodermic involvement.
Large Granular Lymphocytic Leukemia	Two types: CD3+, CD8+T-cells or CD3-, CD2+, CD16+, CD56+ NK cells.	None Specific. The NK variety lacks TCR rearrangements.	Adults with splenomegaly, neutropenia, anemia.